Be
Victorious

New Testament BE Books by Warren Wiersbe

Be Loyal *(Matthew)*
Be Diligent *(Mark)*
Be Compassionate *(Luke 1–13)*
Be Courageous *(Luke 14–24)*
Be Alive *(John 1–12)*
Be Transformed *(John 13–21)*
Be Dynamic *(Acts 1–12)*
Be Daring *(Acts 13–28)*
Be Right *(Romans)*
Be Wise *(1 Corinthians)*
Be Encouraged *(2 Corinthians)*
Be Free *(Galatians)*
Be Rich *(Ephesians)*
Be Joyful *(Philippians)*
Be Complete *(Colossians)*
Be Ready *(1 & 2 Thessalonians)*
Be Faithful *(1 & 2 Timothy, Titus, Philemon)*
Be Confident *(Hebrews)*
Be Mature *(James)*
Be Hopeful *(1 Peter)*
Be Alert *(2 Peter, 2 & 3 John, Jude)*
Be Real *(1 John)*
Be Victorious *(Revelation)*

Be
Victorious

Warren W.
Wiersbe

David C Cook
transforming lives together

BE VICTORIOUS
Published by David C. Cook
4050 Lee Vance View
Colorado Springs, CO 80918 U.S.A.

David C. Cook Distribution Canada
55 Woodslee Avenue, Paris, Ontario, Canada N3L 3E5

David C. Cook U.K., Kingsway Communications
Eastbourne, East Sussex BN23 6NT, England

David C. Cook and the graphic circle C logo
are registered trademarks of Cook Communications Ministries.

Unless otherwise noted, Scripture quotations are taken from the *King James
Version*. Other quotations are taken from the *Holy Bible, New International
Version*® (NIV), © 1973, 1978, 1984 by the International Bible Society, used by
permission of Zondervan Bible Publishers; the *New American Standard Bible*®
(NASB), © The Lockman Foundation 1960, 1962, 1963, 1968, 1971, 1972, 1973,
1975, 1977; J.B. Phillips: *The New Testament in Modern English* (PH), Revised
Edition © J.B. Phillips, 1958, 1960, 1972, permission of Macmillan Publishing Co.
and Collins Publishers; *The New Testament: An Expanded Translation* by Kenneth S.
Wuest (WUEST), © 1961 by Wm. B. Eerdmans Publishing Company.

LCCN 85-50316
ISBN 978-0-89693-547-1

© 1985 by Warren W. Wiersbe

Cover Design: iDesignEtc.
Cover Photo: Brand X Pictures©
Study Questions: Carol Smith

Printed in the United States of America
First Edition 1985

24 25 26 27 28 29

101007

CONTENTS

Dedicated to
our pastor and his wife,
Curt and Claudine Lehman,
whose ministry has helped many
to become overcomers.

PREFACE

The Book of the Revelation of Jesus Christ has challenged and fascinated Bible students for centuries. In my own library, I have dozens of commentaries on this book, and no two authors completely agree on everything.

But this is not important. What is important is that we not miss the major message of Revelation: *the glorious victory of Jesus Christ over all His enemies.* It would be unfortunate for the Bible student to get so lost in the details of this stirring prophecy that he miss its tremendous and overarching truth: *in Jesus Christ, we are overcomers!*

John wrote this book to encourage first-century Christians who were experiencing great suffering. In every age of the church, Revelation has brought comfort and hope. Why? Because its symbols are timeless and may be understood by believers in any period of history; because its promises are eternal and may be trusted by all saints.

I believe that John prophesied about specific events and a specific sequence of events; but I do not want my personal interpretation of prophecy to detour you from the main message of the book: Jesus Christ is the Conqueror, and all believers share in His great victory.

Those students who wish to pursue a more detailed study of Revelation are encouraged to read the commentaries by Lehman Strauss (Loizeaux Brothers), John F. Walvoord (Moody Press), W.A. Criswell (Zondervan), William R. Newell (Moody Press), and Leon Morris (Wm. B. Eerdmans).

Warren W. Wiersbe

1

A Very Special Book

Revelation 1

"Don't ever prophesy," said American humorist Josh Billings, "for if you prophesy wrong, nobody will forget it; and if you prophesy right, nobody will remember it."

Over the centuries, prophecies have come and gone; yet the book that the Apostle John wrote near the close of the first century is with us still. I can recall reading it as a child and wondering what it was all about. Even today, with many years of concentrated study behind me, I am still fascinated by its message and mysteries.

In Revelation 1, John introduces his book and gives us the data essential for appreciating and understanding this prophecy.

The Title (Rev. 1:1a)

The word translated *revelation* simply means "unveiling." It gives us our English word *apocalypse* which, unfortunately, is today a synonym for chaos and catastrophe. The verb simply means "to uncover, to reveal, to make manifest." In this book, the Holy Spirit pulls back the curtain and gives us the privilege of seeing the glorified Christ in heaven and the fulfillment of His sovereign purposes in the world.

In other words, Revelation is an *open* book in which God

reveals His plans and purposes to His church. When Daniel finished writing his prophecy, he was instructed to "shut up the words, and seal the book" (Dan. 12:4); but John was given opposite instructions: "Seal not the sayings of the prophecy of this book" (Rev. 22:10). Why? Since Calvary, the Resurrection, and the coming of the Holy Spirit, God has ushered in the "last days" (Heb. 1:1-2) and is fulfilling His hidden purposes in this world. "The time is at hand" (Rev. 1:3; 22:10).

John's prophecy is primarily the revelation of Jesus Christ, not the revelation of future events. You must not divorce the Person from the prophecy, for without the Person there could be no fulfillment of the prophecy. "He is not incidental to its action," wrote Dr. Merrill Tenney. "He is its chief subject." In Revelation 1—3, Christ is seen as the exalted Priest-King ministering to the churches. In Revelation 4—5, He is seen in heaven as the glorified Lamb of God, reigning on the throne. In Revelation 6—18, Christ is the Judge of all the earth; and in Revelation 19, He returns to earth as the conquering King of kings. The book closes with the heavenly Bridegroom ushering His bride, the church, into the glorious heavenly city.

Whatever you do as you study this book, get to know your Saviour better.

The Author (Rev. 1:1-2, 4, 9; 22:8)
The Holy Spirit used the Apostle John to give us three kinds of inspired literature: the Gospel of John, the three epistles, and the Book of Revelation. His purposes may be outlined as follows:

Gospel of John	Epistles	Revelation
Believe, 20:31	Be sure, 1 John 5:13	Be ready, 22:20
Life received	Life revealed	Life rewarded
Salvation	Sanctification	Sovereignty
The Prophet	The Priest	The King

John wrote Revelation about A.D. 95, during the reign of the Roman emperor Titus Flavius Domitian. The emperor had demanded that he be worshiped as "Lord and God," and the refusal of both Christians and Jews to obey his edict led to severe persecution. Tradition says that it was Domitian who sent John to the Isle of Patmos, a Roman penal colony off the coast of Asia Minor. This being the location of John's exile, perhaps it is not surprising that the word *sea* is found twenty-six times in his book.

During Christ's earthly ministry, John and his brother James asked Jesus for special places of honor by His throne. The Lord told them that they would have to merit their thrones by sharing in His suffering. James was the first apostle martyred (Acts 12:1-2); John was the last of the apostles to die, but he suffered on Patmos before his death. (See Matt. 20:20-23.)

How did the Lord convey the contents of this book to His servant? According to Revelation 1:1-2, the Father gave the revelation to the Son, and the Son shared it with the apostle, using "His angel" as intermediary. Sometimes Christ Himself conveyed information to John (1:10ff); sometimes it was an elder (7:13); and often it was an angel (17:1; 19:9-10). Sometimes a "voice from heaven" told John what to say and do (10:4). The book came from God to John, no matter what the various means of communication were; and it was all inspired by the Spirit.

The word *signified* (1:1) is important; it means "to show by a sign." In Revelation, the noun is translated as *sign* (15:1), *wonder* (12:1, 3), and *miracle* (19:20). This is the same word used in the Gospel of John for the miracles of Jesus Christ, for His miracles were events that carried a deeper spiritual message than simply the display of power. As you study Revelation, expect to encounter a great deal of symbolism, much of it related to the Old Testament.

Why did John use symbolism? For one thing, this kind of "spiritual code" is understood only by those who know Christ personally. If any Roman officers had tried to use

Revelation as evidence against Christians, the book would have been a puzzle and an enigma to them. But an even greater reason is that symbolism is not weakened by time. John was able to draw on the great "images" in God's revelation and assemble them into an exciting drama that has encouraged persecuted and suffering saints for centuries. However, you must not conclude that John's use of symbolism indicates that the events described are not real. They are real!

There is a third reason why John used symbolism: symbols not only convey information, but also impart values and arouse emotions. John could have written, "A dictator will rule the world," but instead he described *a beast.* The symbol says much more than the mere title of "dictator." Instead of explaining a world system, John simply introduced "Babylon the Great" and contrasted the "harlot" with the "bride." The very name "Babylon" would convey deep spiritual truth to readers who knew the Old Testament.

In understanding John's symbolism, however, we must be careful not to allow our imaginations to run wild. Biblical symbols are consistent with the whole of biblical revelation. Some symbols are explained (1:20; 4:5; 5:8); others are understood from Old Testament symbolism (2:7, 17; 4:7); and some symbols are not explained at all (the "white stone" in 2:17). Nearly 300 references to the Old Testament are found in Revelation! This means that we must anchor our interpretations to what God has already revealed, lest we misinterpret this important prophetic book.

The Readers (Rev. 1:3-4)
While the book was originally sent to seven actual local churches in Asia Minor, John makes it clear that *any* believer may read and profit from it (1:3). In fact, God promised a special blessing to the one who would read the book and obey its message. (The verb *read* means "to read out loud." Revelation was first read aloud in local church meetings.) The Apostle Paul had sent letters to seven churches—Rome,

7 = fullness
completeness

Corinth, Galatia, Ephesus, Philippi, Colossae, and Thessalonica—and now John sent one book to seven different churches. Early in the book, he had a special message from Christ to each church.

John did not send this book of prophecy to the assemblies in order to satisfy their curiosity about the future. God's people were going through intense persecution and they needed encouragement. As they heard this book, its message would give them strength and hope. But even more, its message would help them examine their own lives (and each local assembly) to determine those areas needing correction. They were not only to *hear* the Word, but they were also to keep it—that is, guard it as a treasure and practice what it said. The blessing would come, not just by *hearing*, but even more so by *doing* (see James 1:22-25).

It is worth noting that there are seven "beatitudes" in Revelation: 1:3; 14:13; 16:15; 19:9; 20:6; 22:7, 14. The number seven is important in this book because it signifies fullness and completeness. In Revelation, God tells us how He is going to complete His great work and usher in His eternal kingdom. In Revelation, you will find seven seals (5:1), seven trumpets (8:6), seven vials (16:1), seven stars (1:16), and seven lampstands (1:12, 20). Other "sevens" in this book will be discussed as we study.

The special messages to each of the seven churches are given in Revelation 2—3. Some students see in these seven churches a "panorama of church history," from apostolic times (Ephesus) to the apostate days of the twentieth century (Laodicea). While these churches may *illustrate* various stages in the history of the church, that was probably not the main reason why these particular assemblies were selected. Instead, these letters remind us that the exalted Head of the church knows what is going on in each assembly, and that our relationship to Him and His Word determines the life and ministry of the local body.

Keep in mind that the churches in Asia Minor were facing persecution and it was important that they be rightly related to the Lord and to each other. They are pictured as seven separate lampstands, each giving light in a dark world (Phil. 2:15; Matt. 5:14-16). The darker the day, the greater the light must shine; unfortunately situations existed in at least five of these assemblies that required correction if their lights were to shine brightly. As you read Revelation 2—3, note that the Lord always reminded them of who He is, and encouraged them to be "overcomers."

What's more, the promise of Jesus Christ's coming should be to all Christians at all times a motivation for obedience and consecration (1:3, 7; 2:5, 25; 3:3, 11; 22:7, 12, 20; see also 1 John 1:1-3). No believer should study prophecy merely to satisfy his curiosity. When Daniel and John received God's revelations of the future, both fell down as dead men (Rev. 1:17; Dan. 10:7-10). They were overwhelmed! We need to approach this book as wonderers and worshipers, not as academic students.

The Dedication (Rev. 1:4-6)

"If you don't stop writing books," a friend said to me, "you will run out of people to dedicate them to!" I appreciated the compliment, but I did not agree with the sentiment. John had no problem knowing to whom his book should be dedicated! But before he wrote the dedication, he reminded his readers that it was the Triune God who had saved them and would keep them as they faced the fiery trials of suffering.

God the Father is described as the Eternal One (see 1:8; 4:8). All history is part of His eternal plan, including the world's persecution of the church. Next, the Holy Spirit is seen in His fullness, for there are not seven Spirits, but one. The reference here is probably to Isaiah 11:2.

Finally, Jesus Christ is seen in His threefold office as Prophet (faithful witness), Priest (first-begotten from the dead), and King (prince of the kings of the earth). *First-begotten* does not mean "the first one raised from the dead," but "the highest of those raised from the dead." *First-born* is a title of honor (see Rom. 8:29; Col. 1:15, 18).

But of the three Persons of the Trinity, it is to Jesus Christ alone that this book is dedicated. The reasons? Because of what He has done for His people. To begin with, *He loves us* (present tense in most manuscripts). This parallels the emphasis in John's Gospel. He also *washed us from our sins*, or, as some texts read, *freed us* from our sins. This parallels the message of John's epistles (see 1 John 1:5ff). As a grand climax, Christ has *made us a kingdom of priests*, and this is the emphasis of Revelation. Today, Jesus Christ is a Priest-King like Melchizedek (Heb. 7), and we are seated with Him on His throne (Eph. 2:1-10).

In His love, God called Israel to be a kingdom of priests (Ex. 19:1-6), but the Jews failed God and their kingdom was taken from them (Matt. 21:43). Today, God's people (the church) are His kings and priests (1 Peter 2:1-10), exercising spiritual authority and serving God in this world.

The Theme (Rev. 1:7-8)

The overriding theme of the Book of Revelation is the return of Jesus Christ to defeat all evil and to establish His reign. It is definitely a book of victory and His people are seen as "overcomers" (see 2:7, 11, 17, 26; 3:5, 12, 21; 11:7; 12:11; 15:2; 21:7). In his first epistle, John also called God's people "overcomers" (2:13-14; 4:4; 5:4-5). Through eyes of unbelief, Jesus Christ and His church are defeated in this world; but through eyes of faith, He and His people are the true victors. As Peter Marshall once said, "It is better to fail in a cause that will ultimately succeed than to succeed in a cause that will ultimately fail."

The statement in verse 7, "Behold, He cometh with clouds" describes our Lord's return *to the earth*, and is amplified in Revelation 19:11ff. This is not the same as His return *in the air* to catch away His people (1 Thes. 4:13-18; 1 Cor. 15:51ff). When He comes to catch away (rapture) His church, He will come "as a thief" (Rev. 3:3; 16:15) and only those who are born again will see Him (1 John 3:1-3). The event described in Revelation 1:7 will be witnessed by the whole world, and especially by a repentant nation of Israel (see Dan. 7:13; Zech. 12:10-12). It will be public, not secret (Matt. 24:30-31), and will climax the Tribulation period described in Revelation 6—19.

Godly Bible students have not always agreed as to the order of events leading up to the establishment of God's eternal kingdom (Rev. 21—22). I personally believe that the next event on God's calendar is the Rapture, when Christ shall return in the air and take His church to glory. Christ's promise to the church in Revelation 3:10-11 indicates that the church will not go through the Tribulation, and this is further supported by Paul in 1 Thessalonians 1:10; 5:9-10. It is significant to me that there is no mention of the word *church* between Revelation 3:22 and 22:16.

After the church is raptured, the events depicted in Revelation 6—19 will occur: the Tribulation, the rise of the "man of sin," the Great Tribulation (the wrath of God) and the destruction of man-made world government, and then Christ's return to the earth to set up His kingdom. Daniel indicates that this period of worldwide trouble will last seven years (Dan. 9:25-27). Throughout the Book of Revelation, you will find measurements of time that coincide with this seven-year time span (11:2-3; 12:6, 14; 13:5).

The titles given to God in verse 8 make it clear that He is certainly able to work out His divine purposes in human history. *Alpha* and *Omega* are the first and last letters of the Greek alphabet; so, God is at the beginning of all things and also at their end. He is the eternal God (see v. 4), unlimited by time. He is also the Almighty, able to do anything. *Almighty* is a key name for God in Revelation (1:8; 4:8; 11:17; 15:3; 16:7, 14; 19:6, 15; 21:22).

God the Father is called "Alpha and Omega" in Revelation 1:8 and 21:6; but the name also is applied to His Son (1:11; 22:13). This is a strong argument for the deity of Christ. Likewise, the title "the first and the last" goes back to Isaiah (41:4; 44:6; 48:12-13) and is another proof that Jesus is God.

The Occasion (Rev. 1:9-18)

This book was born out of John's profound spiritual experience while exiled on Patmos.

WHAT JOHN HEARD (1:9-11) on that Lord's Day was a trumpetlike voice behind him. It was Jesus Christ speaking! As far as we know, the apostle had not heard his Lord's voice since Christ had returned to heaven more than sixty years before. The Lord commissioned John to write this book and to send it to the seven churches He had selected. Later John would hear another trumpetlike voice, summoning him to heaven (4:1). (Some students relate this to 1 Thessalonians 4:13-18 and see John's "rapture" as a picture of the rapture of the church.)

WHAT JOHN SAW (1:12-16) was a vision of the glorified Christ. Revelation 1:20 makes clear that we must not interpret this vision literally, for it is made up of symbols. The seven lampstands represent the seven churches that would receive the book. Each local church is the bearer of God's light in this dark world. Compare this vision with Daniel's (Dan. 7:9-14).

Christ's garments are those of a Judge-King, One with honor and authority. The white hair symbolizes His eternality, "the Ancient of days" (Dan. 7:9, 13, 22). His eyes see all (Rev. 19:12; Heb. 4:12), enabling Him to judge righteously. His feet of burning brass also suggest judgment, since the brazen altar was the place where the fire consumed the sin offering. The Lord had come to judge the churches, and He would also judge the evil world system.

The "sound of many waters" (v. 15) makes me think of Niagara Falls! Perhaps two ideas are suggested here: (1) Christ gathers together all the "streams of revelation" and is the Father's "last Word" to man (Heb. 1:1-3); (2) He speaks with power and authority and must be heard. The sword from His mouth certainly represents the living Word of God (Heb. 4:12; Eph. 6:17). He fights His enemies by using His Word (Rev. 2:16; 19:19-21).

Verse 20 informs us that the seven stars in His hand represent the angels (*messengers*, see Luke 7:24 where the Greek word is so translated), or perhaps pastors, of the seven churches. God holds His servants and places them where He wants them to "shine" for Him. In Daniel 12:3, wise soul-winners are compared to shining stars.

The Lord's shining countenance reminds us of His transfiguration (Matt. 17:2) and also the prophecy of Malachi 4:2 ("the Sun of righteousness [shall] arise"). The sun is a familiar image of God in the Old Testament (Ps. 84:11), reminding us not only of blessing, but of judgment. The sun can burn as well as bless!

This vision of Christ was totally different in appearance from the Saviour that John knew "in the flesh" when He was ministering on earth. He was not the "gentle Jewish carpenter" that sentimentalists like to sing about. He is the risen, glorified, exalted Son of God, the Priest-King who has the authority to judge all men, beginning with His own people (1 Peter 4:17).

WHAT JOHN DID (1:17-18) was predictable: he fell at the Lord's feet as though he were dead! And this is the apostle that leaned on Jesus' breast! (John 13:23) A vision of the exalted Christ can only produce awe and fear (Dan. 10:7-9). We need this attitude of respect today when so many believers speak and act with undue familiarity toward God. John's response illustrates what Paul wrote in 2 Corinthians 5:16: "Though we have known Christ after the flesh, yet now henceforth know we Him no more." John no longer "nestled" next to the Lord's heart, relating to Him as he had done before.

The Lord reassured John by touching him and speaking to him. (Note Dan. 8:18; 9:21; 10:10, 16, 18.) "Fear not!" is a great encouragement for any child of God. We need not fear life, because He is "The Living One." We need not fear death, because He died and is alive, having conquered death. And we need not fear eternity because He holds the keys of hades (the world of the dead) and of death. The One with the keys is the One who has authority.

At the very beginning of this book, Jesus presented Himself to His people in majestic glory. What the church needs today is a new awareness of Christ and His glory. We need to see Him "high and lifted up" (Isa. 6:1). There is a dangerous absence of awe and worship in our assemblies today. We are boasting about standing on our own feet, instead of breaking and falling at His feet. For years, Evan Roberts prayed, "Bend me! Bend me!" and when God answered, the great Welsh Revival resulted.

The Outline (Rev. 1:19)

To the best of my knowledge, the Book of Revelation is the only book in the Bible that contains an inspired outline of the contents. "The things which thou hast seen" refers to the vision in chapter 1. "The things which are" refers to chapters 2—3, the special messages to the seven churches. "The things which shall be hereafter" covers the events described in chapters 4—22. What John heard in 4:1 substantiates this interpretation.

Here, then, is a suggested outline of the book, based on this interpretation of verse 19:

I. **THE THINGS WHICH THOU HAST SEEN** - ch. 1
   John's vision of the exalted Christ

II. **THE THINGS WHICH ARE** - chs. 2—3
   The messages to the seven churches

III. **THE THINGS WHICH SHALL BE HEREAFTER** - chs. 4—22
   A. The throne in heaven, 4—5
   B. The Tribulation on earth, 6—19
      1. The first half, 6—9
      2. The middle, 10—14
      3. The last half, 15—19
   C. The kingdom of Christ, 20
   D. The new heavens and earth, 21—22

In review, we can summarize the basic characteristics of this remarkable book as follows:

1. It is a Christ-centered book. To be sure, *all* Scripture speaks of the Saviour; but the Book of Revelation especially magnifies the greatness and glory of Jesus Christ. The book is, after all, the revelation of Jesus Christ and not simply the revelation of future events.

2. It is an "open" book. John was told not to seal the book (22:10) because God's people need the message it contains. Revelation *can* be understood, despite the fact that it contains mysteries that may never be comprehended until we meet at the throne of God. John sent the book to the seven churches of Asia Minor with the expectation that, when it was read aloud by the messengers, the listening saints would understand enough of its truths so as to be greatly encouraged in their own difficult situations.

3. It is a book filled with symbols. Biblical symbols are timeless in their message and limitless in their content. For instance, the symbol of "Babylon" originates in Genesis 10—11, and its meaning grows as you trace it through Scripture, climaxing with Revelation 17—18. The same is true of the symbols of "the Lamb" and "the bride." It is exciting to seek to penetrate deeper into the rich meanings that are conveyed by these symbols.

4. It is a book of prophecy. This is definitely stated in Revelation 1:3; 22:7, 10, 18-19; note also 10:11. The letters to the seven churches of Asia Minor dealt with immediate needs in those assemblies, needs that are still with us in churches today; but the rest of the book is devoted almost entirely to prophetic revelations. It was by seeing the victorious Christ presented that the persecuted Christians found encouragement for their difficult task of witnessing. When you have assurance for the future, you have stability in the present. John himself was suffering under the hand of Rome (1:9), so the book was born out of affliction.

5. It is a book with a blessing. We have already noted the promise in Revelation 1:3, as well as the six other "beatitudes" scattered throughout the book. It is not enough simply to hear (or read) the book; we must respond to its message from the heart. We must take the message personally and say a believing "Amen!" to what it says. (Note the many "Amens" in the book: 1:6, 7, 18; 3:14; 5:14; 7:12; 19:4; 22:20-21.)

6. *It is a relevant book.* What John wrote about would "shortly come to pass" (1:1) because "the time is at hand" (1:3). (Note also 22:7, 10, 12, 20.) The word *shortly* does not mean "soon" or "immediately," but "quickly, swiftly." God does not measure time as we do (2 Peter 3:1-10). No one knows when our Lord shall return; but when He begins to open the seals of the scroll (6:1ff), events will occur with speed and without interruption.

7. *It is a majestic book.* Revelation is the book of "the throne," for the word *throne* is found forty-six times throughout. This book magnifies the sovereignty of God. Christ is presented in His glory and dominion!

8. *It is a universal book.* John saw nations and peoples (10:11; 11:9; 17:15) as part of God's program. He also saw the throne room of heaven and heard voices from the ends of the universe!

9. *It is a climactic book.* Revelation is the climax of the Bible. All that began in Genesis will be completed and fulfilled in keeping with God's sovereign will. He is "Alpha and Omega, the beginning and the ending" (1:8). What God starts, He finishes!

But before visiting the throne room of heaven, we must pause to listen to "the Man among the lampstands" as He reveals the personal needs in our churches and in our own hearts. "He that hath an ear, let him hear what the Spirit saith unto the churches!"

2

Christ and the Churches, Part 1

Revelation 2

If you have ever moved to a new community and had to select a new church home, you know how difficult it is to examine and evaluate a church and its ministry. Imposing buildings may house dying or dead congregations, while modest structures might belong to virile assemblies on the march for the Lord. The church we think is "rich" may turn out to be poor in God's sight (Rev. 3:17), while the "poor" church is actually rich! (2:9)

Only the Head of the church, Jesus Christ, can accurately inspect each church and know its true condition, because He sees the internals, not only the externals (2:23b). In these special messages to the seven churches in Asia Minor, the Lord gave each assembly an "X ray" of its condition. But He intended for *all* the churches to read these messages and benefit from them. (Note the plural "churches" in 2:7, 11, 17, 29; 3:6, 13, 22.)

But the Lord was also speaking to *individuals*, and this is where you and I come in. "He that hath an ear, let him hear." Churches are made up of individuals, and it is individuals who determine the spiritual life of the assembly. So, while reading these messages, we must apply them personally as we examine our own hearts.

Finally, we must keep in mind that John was a pastor at heart, seeking to encourage these churches during a difficult time of persecution. Before Christ judges the world, He must judge His own people (1 Peter 4:17; Ezek. 9:6). A purified church need never fear the attacks of Satan or men. "It is a very remarkable thing," wrote G. Campbell Morgan, "that the church of Christ persecuted has been the church of Christ pure. The church of Christ patronized has always been the church of Christ impure."

Ephesus, the Careless Church (Rev. 2:1-7)

Each of the seven messages begins with a personal description or designation of Jesus Christ taken from the vision of Christ given in Revelation 1. (In the case of Ephesus, see 1:12, 16, 20.) The Ephesian assembly had enjoyed some "stellar" leadership—Paul, Timothy, and the Apostle John himself—but the Lord reminded them that *He* was in control of the ministry, placing the "stars" where He pleased. How easy it is for a church to become proud and forget that pastors and teachers are God's gifts (Eph. 4:11) who may be taken away at any time. Some churches need to be cautioned to worship the Lord and not their pastor!

APPROVAL (2:2-3, 6). How gracious of the Lord to start with words of commendation! To begin with, this was a *serving* church, busy doing the works of the Lord. No doubt their weekly schedule was filled with activities. It was also a *sacrificing* church, for the word *labor* means "toil to the point of exhaustion." The Ephesian Christians paid a price to serve the Lord. They were a *steadfast* assembly, for the word *patience* carries the meaning of "endurance under trial." They kept going when the going was tough.

The Ephesian church was a *separated* people, for they carefully examined the visiting ministers (see 2 John 7-11) to see if they were genuine. Paul had warned the Ephesian elders that false teachers would come in from the outside and even arise from within the church (Acts 20:28-31), and John had instructed them to "try the spirits" (1 John 4:1-6).

Indeed, Satan has his false ministers and the church must be constantly alert to detect them and reject them (2 Cor. 11:1-4, 12-15).

Ephesian Christians separated themselves not only from false doctrine but also from false deeds (Rev. 2:6). The word *Nicolaitane* means "to conquer the people." Some Bible students believe this was a sect who "lorded it over" the church and robbed the people of their liberty in Christ (see 3 John 9-11). They initiated what we know today as "clergy" and "laity," a false division that is taught nowhere in the New Testament. All God's people are "kings and priests" (Rev. 1:6; 1 Peter 2:9) and have equal access to the Father through the blood of Christ (Heb. 10:19ff). We shall meet this dangerous sect again when we study the message to the church at Pergamos.

The believers at Ephesus were a *suffering* people who patiently bore their burdens and toiled without fainting. And they did all of this for His name's sake! No matter how you examine this congregation, you conclude that it is just about perfect. However, the One among the lampstands saw into their hearts, and He had a different diagnosis from ours.

ACCUSATION (2:4). This busy, separated, sacrificing church really suffered from "heart trouble"—they had abandoned their first love! They displayed "works . . . labor . . . and patience" (Rev. 2:2), but these qualities were not motivated by a love for Christ. (Compare 1 Thes. 1:3—"work of faith, and labor of love, and patience of hope.") What we do for the Lord is important, *but so is why we do it!*

What is "first love"? It is the devotion to Christ that so often characterizes the new believer: fervent, personal, uninhibited, excited, and openly displayed. It is the "honeymoon love" of the husband and wife (Jer. 2:1-2). While it is true that mature married love deepens and grows richer, it is also true that it should never lose the excitement and wonder of those "honeymoon days." When a husband and wife begin to take each other for granted, and life becomes routine, then the marriage is in danger.

Just think of it: it is possible to serve, sacrifice, and suffer "for My name's sake" and yet not really love Jesus Christ! The Ephesian believers were so busy maintaining their separation that they were neglecting adoration. Labor is no substitute for love; neither is purity a substitute for passion. The church must have both if it is to please Him.

By reading Paul's epistle to the Ephesians, you discover at least twenty references to *love*. You also discover that Paul emphasized the believer's exalted position "in Christ . . . in the heavenly places." But the Ephesian church had fallen and was not living up to its heavenly position in Christ (Rev. 2:5). It is only as we love Christ fervently that we can serve Him faithfully. Our love for Him must be pure (Eph. 6:24).

ADMONITION (2:5-7). "First love" can be restored if we follow the three instructions Christ gave. First, we must *remember* (literally "keep on remembering") what we have lost and cultivate a desire to regain that close communion once again. Then we must *repent*—change our minds—and confess our sins to the Lord (1 John 1:9). Third, we must *repeat the first works*, which suggests restoring the original fellowship that was broken by our sin and neglect. For the believer, this means prayer, Bible reading and meditation, obedient service, and worship.

In spite of the privileges it had enjoyed, the church of Ephesus was in danger of losing its light! The church that loses its love will soon lose its light, no matter how doctrinally sound it may be. "I will come" (Rev. 2:5) is not referring to the Lord's return, but to His coming judgment *then and there*. The glorious city of Ephesus is today but a heap of stones and no light is shining there.

Verse 7 makes it clear that individual believers within the church may be true to the Lord, no matter what others may do. In these seven messages, the "overcomers" are not a "spiritual elite," but rather the true believers whose faith has given them victory (1 John 5:4-5). Sinful man was banned from the tree of life (Gen. 3:22-24), but in Christ we have eternal abundant life (John 3:16; 10:10). We enjoy this bless-

ing now, and we shall enjoy it in greater measure in eternity
(Rev. 22:1-5).

The church of Ephesus was the "careless church," made
up of careless believers who neglected their love for Christ.
Are we guilty of the same neglect?

Smyrna, the Crowned Church (Rev. 2:8-11)

The name *Smyrna* means "bitter" and is related to the word
myrrh. The city remains a functioning community today
called Izmir. The assembly at Smyrna was persecuted for the
faith, which explains why the Lord emphasized His death
and resurrection as He opened His message. No matter what
experiences God's people may have, their Lord identifies
with them.

APPROVAL (2:9). The church at Smyrna was not having an
easy time of it! The members were persecuted, probably
because they refused to compromise and say, "Caesar is
Lord." Smyrna was an important center of the Roman imperial cult, and anyone refusing to acknowledge Caesar as Lord
would certainly be excluded from the guilds. This would
mean unemployment and poverty. The word used here for
poverty means "abject poverty, possessing absolutely nothing."

A large Jewish community also thrived in Smyrna. The
Jews, of course, did not have to patronize the imperial cult
since their religion was accepted by Rome; but they certainly
would not cooperate with the Christian faith. So, from both
Jews and Gentiles, the Christians in Smyrna received slander
and suffering.

But they were rich! They lived for eternal values that
would never change, riches that could never be taken away.
"As poor, yet making many rich" (2 Cor. 6:10; 8:9). In fact,
their suffering for Christ only increased their riches.

Our struggles are not with flesh and blood, but with the
enemy, Satan, who uses people to accomplish his purposes.
The Jewish synagogue was actually a synagogue of Satan. A
true Jew is not one physically or racially, but spiritually

(Rom. 2:17-29). Any religious group, Jewish or Gentile, that does not acknowledge Jesus Christ as God's Son is certainly acting contrary to God's will.

ADMONITION (2:10-11). No words of accusation are given to the congregation in Smyrna! They may not have enjoyed the approval of men, but they certainly received the praise of God. However, the Lord did give them solemn words of admonition as they faced increased suffering: "Don't be afraid!"

He assured them that He knew the devil's plans and was in complete control of the situation. Some of the believers would be imprisoned and tried as traitors to Rome. Yet their tribulation would not be long; in the Bible, *ten days* signifies "a brief time" (Gen. 24:55; Acts 25:6). The important thing was *faithfulness*, standing true to Christ no matter what the government might threaten to do.

The "crown of life" is the winner's crown awarded at the annual athletic games. Smyrna was a key participant in the games, so this promise would be especially meaningful to believers living there. The Lord reinforced the promise given by James (James 1:12) and assured His people that there was nothing to fear. Because they had trusted Him, they were overcomers—victors in the race of faith (Heb. 12:1-3)—and, as overcomers, they had nothing to fear. Even if they were martyred, they would be ushered into glory, wearing crowns! They would never face the awful judgment of the second death, which is the lake of fire (Rev. 20:14; 21:8).

It costs to be a dedicated Christian, in some places more than others. As end-time pressures increase, persecution will also increase; and God's people need to be ready (1 Peter 4:12ff). The world may call us "poor Christians," but in God's sight we are rich!

Pergamos, the Compromising Church (Rev. 2:12-17)

Called "the greatest city in Asia Minor," Pergamos had the first temple dedicated to Caesar and was a rabid promoter of the imperial cult. This is probably what is meant by

"Satan's seat" in verse 13. The city also had a temple dedicated to Aesculapius, the god of healing, whose insignia was the entwined serpent on the staff. (This is still a medical symbol today.) Satan, of course, is likewise symbolized as the serpent (2 Cor. 11:3; Rev. 12:9; 20:2).

APPROVAL (2:13). Like their brothers and sisters in Smyrna, the believers in Pergamos had suffered persecution, and one of their men had died for the faith. In spite of intense suffering, this church had remained true to God. They refused to drop incense on the altar and say, "Caesar is Lord." The Lord's description of Himself ("He which hath the sharp sword," v. 12) would surely encourage the people, for the sword was also the symbol of the Roman proconsul. It was more important that the church fear Christ's sword than the Roman sword! (v. 16)

ACCUSATION (2:14-15). Despite their courageous stand against persecution, the believers in Pergamos were not faultless before the Lord. Satan had not been able to destroy them by coming as the roaring lion (1 Peter 5:8), but he was making inroads as the deceiving serpent. A group of compromising people had infiltrated the church fellowship, and Jesus Christ hated their doctrines and their practices.

These infiltrators are called "Nicolaitanes," whom we met already at Ephesus (2:6). The name means "to rule the people." What they taught is called "the doctrine of Balaam" (2:14). The Hebrew name *Balaam* also means "lord of the people" and is probably synonymous with *Nicolaitanes*. Sadly, this group of professed believers "lorded it over" the people and led them astray.

Understanding the story of Balaam helps us interpret this insidious group more accurately. (See Num. 22—25.) Balaam was a true prophet who prostituted his gifts in order to earn money from King Balak, who hired him to curse the people of Israel. God prevented Balaam from actually cursing the nation—in fact, God turned the curses into blessings!—but Balak still got his money's worth. How? By following Balaam's advice and making friends with Israel, and then inviting the Jews to worship and feast at the pagan altars. "If you can't beat 'em, join 'em!"

The Jewish men fell right into the trap and many of them became "good neighbors." They ate meat from idolatrous altars and committed fornication as part of heathen religious rites. Twenty-four thousand people died because of this disobedient act of compromise (Num. 25:1-9).

Why did this bit of ancient history apply to the believers at Pergamos? Because a group in that church said, "There is nothing wrong with being friendly to Rome. What harm is there in putting a pinch of incense on the altar and affirming your loyalty to Caesar?" Antipas refused to compromise and was martyred; but others took the "easy way" and cooperated with Rome.

It is unlikely that "things sacrificed to idols" is the same problem Paul dealt with in 1 Corinthians 8 and 10. The accusation here left no room for personal choice as did Paul. The Lord accused the Christians in Pergamos of sinning, of committing "spiritual fornication" by saying, "Caesar is Lord." Of course, this compromise made them welcome in the Roman guilds and protected them from Roman persecution, but it cost them their testimony and their crown.

Believers today also face the temptation to achieve personal advancement by ungodly compromise. The name *Pergamos* means "married," reminding us that each local church is "engaged to Christ" and must be kept pure (2 Cor. 11:1-4). We shall see later in Revelation that this present world system is pictured as a defiled harlot, while the church is presented as a pure bride. The congregation or the individual Christian that compromises with the world just to avoid suffering or achieve success is committing "spiritual adultery" and being unfaithful to the Lord.

ADMONITION (2:16-17). Antipas had felt the sword of Rome, but the church at Pergamos would feel the sword of Christ —the Word (Heb. 4:12)—if they did not repent. This is not a reference to our Lord's return but to a *present* judgment that comes to a church when it is disobedient to the Word of

God. The Lord had presented Himself as "He which hath the sharp sword" (Rev. 2:12), so the church could not have been ignorant of its danger.

As with the previous churches, the closing appeal is to *the individual:* "*He* that hath an ear. . . . To *him* that overcometh" (v. 17, italics added). God fed the Israelites with manna during their wilderness travels, and a pot of the manna was placed in the ark of the covenant (Ex. 16:32-36; Heb. 9:4). Instead of eating "things sacrificed to idols" (Rev. 2:14), the believers in Pergamos needed to feast on God's holy food, the bread of life found in Jesus Christ through the Word (John 6:32ff; Matt. 4:4). The ark of the covenant was the throne of God (2 Sam. 6:2; Isa. 37:16; Ps. 80:1; all NASB), in contrast to Satan's throne which held authority in Pergamos (Rev. 2:13).

In those days, a white stone was put into a vessel by a judge to vote acquittal for a person on trial. It was also used like a "ticket" to gain admission to a feast. Both would certainly apply to the believer in a spiritual sense: he has been declared righteous through faith in Christ, and he feasts with Christ today (3:20) and will feast with Him in glory (19:6-9).

Thyatira, the Corrupted Church (Rev. 2:18-29)

The longest message was sent to the church in the smallest city! Thyatira was a military town as well as a commercial center with many trade guilds. Wherever guilds were found, idolatry and immorality—the two great enemies of the early church—were almost always present too.

The city boasted a special temple to Apollo, the "sun god," which explains why the Lord introduced Himself as "the Son of God" (the only time in Revelation this title is used). John had to deliver a message of severe warning and judgment to this congregation, which explains the description of the Lord's eyes and feet.

APPROVAL (2:19). The believers in Thyatira were a busy lot! They were involved in sacrificial ministry for the sake of others. What's more, their works were increasing and characterized by faith, love, and patience; so the church was not guilty of mere "religious activity."

ACCUSATION (2:20-23). Alas, the Lord found much to expose and condemn in the assembly at Thyatira. No amount of loving and sacrificial works can compensate for tolerance of evil. The church was permitting a false prophetess to influence the people and lead them into compromise. It is not likely that this woman was actually called "Jezebel," since such an infamous name would not be given to a child. The name is symbolic: Jezebel was the idolatrous queen who enticed Israel to add Baal worship to their religious ceremonies. (See 1 Kings 16—19.) The seductive teaching of Jezebel was similar to the "doctrine of Balaam" that the Lord condemned in the church of Pergamos (Rev. 2:14). She taught believers how to compromise with the Roman religion and the practices of the guilds, so that Christians would not lose their jobs or their lives.

It is interesting to contrast the churches at Ephesus and Thyatira. The Ephesian church was weakening in its love, yet faithful to judge false teachers; while the people in the assembly at Thyatira were growing in their love, but too tolerant of false doctrine. Both extremes must be avoided in the church. "Speaking the truth in love" is the biblical balance (Eph. 4:15). Unloving orthodoxy and loving compromise are both hateful to God.

Not only was the church at Thyatira tolerant of evil, but it was proud and unwilling to repent. The Lord gave the false prophetess time to repent, yet she refused. Now He was giving her followers opportunity to repent. His eyes of fire had searched out their thoughts and motives, and He would make no mistake.

In fact, the Lord threatened to use this assembly as a solemn example to "all the churches" not to tolerate evil. Jezebel and her children (followers) would be sentenced to tribulation and death! Idolatry and compromise are, in the Bible, pictured as fornication and unfaithfulness to the marriage vows (Jer. 3:6ff; Hosea 9:1ff). Jezebel's bed of sin would become a bed of sickness! To *kill with death* means "to kill with pestilence" (see NASB). God would judge the false prophetess and her followers once and for all.

ADMONITION (2:24-29). Not everyone in the assembly was unfaithful to the Lord, and He had a special word for them. They had separated themselves from the false doctrine and compromising practices of Jezebel and her followers, which Christ denounces as "the depths of Satan" (note the contrast in 1 Cor. 2:10). The Lord had no special demands to make; He simply wanted them to hold fast in their resistance to evil. "Till I come" refers to Christ's return for His people, at which time He will reward them for their faithfulness (see 3:3; 16:15; 22:7, 17, 20). This is the first mention in Revelation of the Lord's coming for the church, the event we commonly call the Rapture (see 1 Thes. 4:13-18). In contrast, the reference in Revelation 1:7 is to Christ's return to earth in judgment, to defeat His enemies and establish His kingdom (see Rev. 19:11ff).

The believers in Thyatira are promised authority over the nations, which probably refers to the fact that God's people will live and reign with Christ (see 20:4). When the Lord sets up His kingdom on earth, it will be a righteous kingdom with perfect justice. He will rule with a rod of iron! (Ps. 2:8-9) Rebellious men will be like clay pots, easily broken to pieces!

Jesus Christ is "the bright and morning star" (Rev. 22:16). The promise in verse 28 suggests that God's people shall be so closely identified with Christ that He will "belong" to them! But perhaps there is also an allusion here to Satan, who wanted the kingdom for himself and who offered the world's kingdoms to Christ if He would worship him but once (Matt. 4:8-11). In Isaiah 14:12, Satan is named *Lucifer*, which in Hebrew means "brightness, bright star." The compromising people in Thyatira were following "the depths of Satan," which would lead to darkness and death. God's overcomers, on the other hand, would share the morning star!

As you review these first four messages to the churches, you can see the dangers that still exist for the people of God. Like Ephesus, we can be zealous and orthodox, but at the same time lose our devotion to Christ. Or, like Thyatira, our love can be increasing yet lacking in the kind of discernment that is necessary to keep the church pure (see Phil. 1:9-11). Like Pergamos and Thyatira, we may be so tolerant of evil that we grieve the Lord and invite His judgment.

Would we have selected Smyrna as the most spiritual church of the four? Probably not, yet the Lord did! We need to remind ourselves not to judge God's people by wrong standards, because only the Lord can see the heart (see 1 Cor. 4:5).

God's exhortation to these churches (except Smyrna) is, "Repent! Change your minds!" It is not only lost sinners who need to repent, but also disobedient Christians. If we do not repent and deal with sin in our lives and in our assemblies, the Lord may judge us and remove our lampstand (Rev. 2:5). How tragic it is when a local church gradually abandons the faith and loses its witness for Christ!

"He that hath an ear, let him hear what the Spirit saith unto the churches!"

3

Christ and the Churches, Part 2

Revelation 3

We are still listening to what the Holy Spirit has to say to the churches; for these messages from Christ belong to our day as well as to the first century. Churches are people, and human nature has not changed. So, as we continue our study, we must not look upon these letters as ancient relics. On the contrary, they are mirrors in which we see ourselves!

Sardis, the Feeble Church (Rev. 3:1-6)

Ancient Sardis, the capital of Lydia, was a most important city. It lay about fifty miles east of Ephesus at the junction of five main roads; so it was a center for trade. It was also a military center, for it was located on an almost inaccessible plateau. The acropolis of Sardis was about 1,500 feet above the main roads, and it formed an impregnable fortress. The main religion in the city was the worship of Artemis, one of the "nature cults" that built on the idea of death and rebirth.

Sardis was also known for its manufacture of woolen garments, a fact that has bearing on Christ's message to the church. Sad to say, the city at that time was but a shadow of its former splendor; and the church, unfortunately, had become like the city—it was alive in name only.

The message to Sardis is a warning to all "great churches" that are living on past glory. Dr. Vance Havner has frequently reminded us that spiritual ministries often go through four stages: a man, a movement, a machine, and then a monument. Sardis was at the "monument" stage, but there was still hope!

There was hope because Christ was the Head of the church and He was able to bring new life. He described Himself as the one possessing the seven Spirits and the seven stars. There is only one Holy Spirit (Eph. 4:4), but the number seven demonstrates fullness and completeness. The Holy Spirit gives life to the church, and life is exactly what the people at Sardis needed. The sevenfold Spirit of God is pictured as seven burning lamps (Rev. 4:5) and as seven all-seeing eyes (5:6).

All of the church's man-made programs can never bring life, any more than a circus can resurrect a corpse. The church was born when the Spirit of God descended on the Day of Pentecost (Acts 2), and its life comes from the Spirit. When the Spirit is grieved, the church begins to lose life and power. When sin is confessed and church members get right with God and with each other, then the Spirit infuses new life—revival!

Christ also controls the seven stars, the messengers of the churches (Rev. 1:20), referring most likely to the pastors. Sometimes it is a pastor's fault that a church is dying, and the Lord of the church must remove the star and put another in his place.

There are no words of commendation to the believers at Sardis. Nor did the Lord point out any doctrinal problems that required correction. Neither is there any mention of opposition or persecution. The church would have been better off had there been some suffering, for it had grown comfortable and content and was living on its past reputation. There was reputation without reality, form without force. Like the city itself, the church at Sardis gloried in past splendor, but ignored present decay.

In fact, even what they did have was about to die! Why? Because the believers had gone to sleep. Twice in its long history, the citadel at Sardis had been captured, each time because sentries had failed to do their jobs faithfully. It is when the church's leaders and members get accustomed to their blessings and complacent about their ministry that the enemy finds his way in.

The impression is that the assembly in Sardis was not aggressive in its witness to the city. There was no persecution because there was no invasion of the enemy's territory. No friction usually means no motion! The unsaved in Sardis saw the church as a respectable group of people who were neither dangerous nor desirable. They were decent people with a dying witness and a decaying ministry.

Our Lord's counsel to the church began with, "Be watchful! Wake up!" (See Rom. 13:11ff.) The "sentries" were asleep! The first step toward renewal in a dying church is honest awareness that something is wrong. When an organism is alive, there is growth, repair, reproduction, and power; if these elements are lacking in a church, then that church is either dying or already dead.

The Lord warned the Ephesian saints that He would come and remove their lampstand if they did not repent (Rev. 2:5). He warned the church at Pergamos that He would come and make war with the sword of the Spirit (2:16). If the believers at Sardis did not follow His orders, He would come as a thief, when they least expected Him; and this would mean judgment.

However, a remnant of dedicated people often exists in even a dying church. The Christians at Sardis had life, even though it was feeble. They were working, even though their works were not all that they could have been. The Lord admonished them to strengthen what remained and not to give up because the church was weak. Where there is life, there is hope!

What was different about this dedicated remnant? They had not defiled their garments (v. 4). There is some evidence from antiquity that temple worshipers were not permitted to approach their gods and goddesses wearing dirty garments. The remnant in the church at Sardis had not compromised with the pagan society around them, nor had they grown comfortable and complacent. It was this devoted spiritual remnant that held the future of the church's ministry.

"Wake up! Be watchful! Repent! Remember the Word you have received and obey it!" This is the formula for revival. It is good to guard our spiritual heritage, but we must not embalm it. It is not enough to be true to the faith and have a great history. That faith must produce life and works.

The promise in verse 5 ("clothed in white raiment") would have been especially meaningful to people who lived in a city where woolen garments were manufactured. And the statement about the names being blotted out would also be significant to people in the Roman Empire, where citizenship was vitally important (see Acts 22:24-30).

Is there a warning here that a true believer might lose his salvation? I don't think so. It would appear that God's "book of life" contains the names of all the living, the wicked as well as the righteous (Ps. 69:28). Revelation 13:8 and 17:8 suggest that the names of the saved are written in the book from the foundation of the world—that is, before they had done anything good or bad. By God's grace, they have been chosen in Christ before the beginning of time (Eph. 1:4; see also Matt. 25:34).

Jesus told His disciples to rejoice because their names were "written in heaven" (Luke 10:20). The Greek verb is in the perfect tense, which means it can be translated (as Kenneth Wuest does in his *Expanded Translation*), "your names have been written in heaven and are on permanent record up there." It is not likely that Jesus would contradict Himself in this important matter!

If the names of believers (the elect) are written from the foundation of the world, and if God knows all things, why would He enter the name of somebody who would one day fall and have to be removed from the book? We are enrolled in heaven because we have been born again (Heb. 12:23), and no matter how disobedient a child may be, he or she cannot be "unborn."

As unbelievers die, their names are removed from the book; thus, at the final judgment, the book contains only the names of believers (Rev. 20:12-15). It then becomes "the Lamb's Book of Life" (21:27), because only those saved by the Lord Jesus Christ have their names in it. All the others have been blotted out, something God would never do for any true child of God (see Ex. 32:32; Rom. 9:3). It is a book of *life*, and lost sinners are *dead*! (Eph. 2:1)

The warning here is that we not grow comfortable in our churches, lest we find ourselves slowly dying. The encouragement is that no church is beyond hope as long as there is a dedicated remnant in it, willing to strengthen the things that remain.

Philadelphia, the Faithful Church (Rev. 3:7-13)

As most people know, *Philadelphia* means "love of the brethren." Certainly, brotherly love is an important mark of the Christian. We are "taught of God to love one another" (1 Thes. 4:9): by God the Father (1 John 4:19), God the Son (John 13:34), and God the Spirit (Rom. 5:5). But it is not enough to love God and our fellow believers; we must also love a .lost world and seek to reach unbelievers with the Good News of the Cross. This church had a vision to reach a lost world, and God set before them an open door.

Philadelphia was situated in a strategic place on the main route of the Imperial Post from Rome to the East, and thus was called "the gateway to the East." It was also called "little Athens" because of the many temples in the city. The church was certainly located in a place of tremendous opportunity.

The only major problem with the location was that the area was prone to earthquakes. Philadelphia sat on a geological fault, and in 17 B.C. it was destroyed by a severe earthquake that also destroyed Sardis and ten other cities. After ward, some of the citizens refused to move back into the city and remained in the surrounding countryside, which they called "the burnt land." There did not seem to be much security in the city of brotherly love!

Jesus Christ presented Himself to the church at Philadelphia as "He that is holy." This is tantamount to declaring that He is God, which, of course, He is. Jesus Christ is holy in His character, His words, His actions, and His purposes. As the Holy One, He is uniquely set apart from everything else, and nothing can be compared to Him.

But He is also the One who is true—that is, genuine. He is the original, not a copy; the authentic God and not a manufactured one. There were hundreds of false gods and goddesses in those days (1 Cor. 8:5-6), but only Jesus Christ could rightfully claim to be the true God.

It is worth noting that when the martyrs in heaven addressed the Lord, they called Him "holy and true" (Rev. 6:10). Their argument was that, because He was holy, He had to judge sin, and because He was true, He had to vindicate His people who had been wickedly slain.

Not only is He holy and true, but He has the authority to open and close doors. The background of this imagery is Isaiah 22:15-25. Assyria had invaded Judah (as Isaiah had warned), but the Jewish leaders were trusting Egypt, not God, to deliver the nation. One of the treacherous leaders was a man named Shebna who had used his office, not for the good of the people, but for his own private gain. God saw to it that Shebna was removed from office and that a faithful man, Eliakim, was put in his place and given the keys of authority. Eliakim was a picture of Jesus Christ, a dependable administrator of the affairs of God's people. Jesus Christ also has the keys of hades and of death (Rev. 1:18).

In the New Testament, an "open door" speaks of opportunity for ministry (Acts 14:27; 1 Cor. 16:9; 2 Cor. 2:12; Col. 4:3). Christ is the Lord of the harvest and the Head of the church, and it is He who determines where and when His people shall serve. (See Acts 16:6-10.) He gave the church at Philadelphia a great opportunity for ministry.

But could they take advantage of it? There were at least two obstacles to overcome, the first being their own lack of strength (Rev. 3:8). Apparently, this was not a large or a strong church; however, it was a faithful one. They were true to God's Word and unafraid to bear His name. Verse 10 suggests that they had endured some special testing and had proved faithful.

It is not the size or strength of a church that determines its ministry, but faith in the call and command of the Lord. "God's commandments are God's enablements." If Jesus Christ gave them an open door, then He would see to it that they were able to walk through it! Martin Luther put it perfectly in his well-known hymn:

> Did we in our own strength confide,
> Our striving would be losing.
> Were not the right Man on our side,
> The Man of God's own choosing.

The second obstacle was the opposition of the Jews in the city (v. 9). This was really the opposition of Satan, for we do not battle against flesh and blood (Eph. 6:12). These people may have been Jews in the flesh, but they were not "true Israel" in the New Testament sense (Rom. 2:17-29). Jewish people certainly have a great heritage, but it is no guarantee of salvation (Matt. 3:7-12; John 8:33ff).

How were these Jews opposing the church at Philadelphia? For one thing, by excluding Jewish believers from the synagogue. Another weapon was probably false accusation, for this is the way the unbelieving Jews often attacked Paul. Satan is the accuser and he uses even religious people to assist him (Rev. 12:10). It is not easy to witness for Christ when the leading people in the community are spreading lies about you. The church at Smyrna faced the same kind of opposition (2:9).

The believers in Philadelphia were in a similar situation to that of Paul when he wrote 1 Corinthians 16:9—there were both opportunities and obstacles! Unbelief sees the obstacles, but faith sees the opportunities! And since the Lord holds the keys, He is in control of the outcome! So what do we have to fear? Nobody can close the doors as long as He keeps them open. Fear, unbelief, and delay have caused the church to miss many God-given opportunities.

The Saviour gave three wonderful and encouraging promises to this church. First, He would take care of their enemies (Rev. 3:9). One day, these people would have to acknowledge that the Christians were right! (See Isa. 60:14; Phil. 2:10-11.) If we take care of God's work, He will take care of our battles.

Second, He would keep them from tribulation (Rev. 3:10). This is surely a reference to the time of tribulation that John described in chapters 6—19, "the time of Jacob's trouble." This is not speaking about some local trial, because it involves "them that dwell on the earth." (See 6:10; 8:13; 11:10; 12:12; 13:8, 12, 14; 14:6; 17:2, 8.) The immediate reference would be to the official Roman persecutions that would come, but the ultimate reference is to the Tribulation that will encompass the earth before Jesus Christ returns to establish His kingdom. In many Bible scholars' understanding, verse 10 is a promise that the church will not endure the Tribulation, but will be taken to heaven before it begins. (See 1 Thes. 4:13—5:11.) The admonition, "Behold, I come quickly," would strengthen this view.

The third promise to the Philadelphians is that God would honor them (Rev. 3:12). The symbolism in this verse would be especially meaningful to people who lived in constant danger of earthquakes: the stability of the pillar, no need to go out or to flee, a heavenly city that nothing could destroy. Ancient cities often honored great leaders by erecting pillars with their names inscribed on them. God's pillars are not made of stone, because there is no temple in the heavenly city (21:22). His pillars are faithful people who bear His name for His glory (Gal. 2:9).

In a very real sense, the church today is like the Philadelphian church, for God has set before us many open doors of opportunity. If He opens the doors, we must work; if He shuts the doors, we must wait. Above all, we must be faithful to Him and see the opportunities, not the obstacles. If we miss our opportunities, we lose our rewards (crowns), and this means being ashamed before Him when He comes (1 John 2:28).

Laodicea, the Foolish Church (Rev. 3:14-22)

As with some of the previous churches, the Lord adapted His words to something significant about the city in which the assembly was located. In this case, Laodicea was known for its wealth and its manufacture of a special eye salve, as well as of a glossy black wool cloth. It also was located near Hieropolis, where there were famous hot springs, and Colossae, known for its pure, cold water.

The Lord presented Himself as "the Amen," which is an Old Testament title for God (see Isa. 65:16, where the word *truth* is the Hebrew word *amen*). He is the truth and speaks the truth, because He is "the faithful and true witness" (Rev. 3:14). The Lord was about to tell this church the truth about its spiritual condition; unfortunately, they would not believe His diagnosis.

"Why is it that new Christians create problems in the church?" a young pastor once asked me.

"They don't create problems," I replied. "They *reveal* them. The problems have always been there, but we've gotten used to them. New Christians are like children in the home: they tell the truth about things!"

The Laodicean church was blind to its own needs and unwilling to face the truth. Yet honesty is the beginning of true blessing, as we admit what we are, confess our sins, and receive from God all that we need. If we want God's best for our lives and churches, we must be honest with God and let God be honest with us.

"The beginning of the creation of God" (v. 14) does not suggest that Jesus was created, and therefore not eternal God. The word translated *beginning* means "source, origin." (See John 1:3; Col. 1:15, 18.)

The Lord demonstrated four areas of need in the church at Laodicea:

THEY HAD LOST THEIR VIGOR (3:16-17). In the Christian life, there are three "spiritual temperatures": a burning heart, on fire for God (Luke 24:32); a cold heart (Matt. 24:12), and a lukewarm heart (Rev. 3:16). The lukewarm Christian is comfortable, complacent, and does not realize his need. If he were cold, at least he would feel it! Both the cold water from Colossae and the hot water from Hieropolis would be lukewarm by the time it was piped to Laodicea.

As believers in Jesus Christ, we have every reason to be "fervent in spirit" (Rom. 12:11). Fervent prayer is also vital (Col. 4:12). It was as the Emmaus disciples listened to the Word that their hearts were warmed. No wonder Paul commanded that his letter to Colossae be sent to the Laodicean church! (Col. 4:16)

We enjoy a beverage that is either hot or cold, but one that is tepid is flat and stale. That's why the waitress keeps adding hot coffee or fresh iced tea to our cups and glasses. The second law of thermodynamics requires that a "closed system" eventually moderates so that no more energy is being produced. Unless something is added from the outside, the system decays and dies. Without added fuel, the hot water in the boiler becomes cool; without electricity, the refrigerant in the freezer becomes warm.

The church cannot be a "closed system." Jesus said, "Without Me ye can do nothing" (John 15:5). The Laodicean church was independent, self-satisfied, and secure. "We have need of nothing!" But all the while, their spiritual power had been decaying; their material wealth and glowing statistics were but shrouds hiding a rotting corpse. Their Lord was *outside the church*, trying to get in! (Rev. 3:20)

THEY HAD LOST THEIR VALUES (3:17-18a). The church at

Smyrna thought itself poor, when it was really rich (2:9); the Laodiceans boasted that they were rich, when in fact they were poor. Perhaps we have here a hint of why this church declined spiritually: they had become proud of their ministry and had begun to measure things by human standards instead of by spiritual values. They were, in the eyes of the Lord, "wretched, and miserable, and poor."

Laodicea was a wealthy city and a banking center. Perhaps some of the spirit of the marketplace crept into the church so that their values became twisted. Why is it that so many church bulletins and letterheads show pictures of *buildings?* Are these the things that are most important to us? The board at the Laodicean church could proudly show you the latest annual report with its impressive statistics; yet Jesus said He was about to vomit them out of His mouth!

The solution? Pay the price to get true "gold tried in the fire." This suggests that the church needed some persecution; they were too comfortable (1 Peter 1:7). Nothing makes God's people examine their priorities faster than suffering!

THEY HAD LOST THEIR VISION (3:18b). The Laodiceans were "blind." They could not see reality. They were living in a fool's paradise, proud of a church that was about to be rejected. The Apostle Peter teaches that when a believer is not growing in the Lord, his spiritual vision is affected (2 Peter 1:5-9). "Diet" has bearing on the condition of one's eyes, in a spiritual sense as well as a physical one.

These people could not see themselves as they really were. Nor could they see their Lord, as He stood outside the door of the church. Nor could they see the open doors of opportunity. They were so wrapped up in building their own kingdom that they had become lukewarm in their concern for a lost world.

The solution? Apply the heavenly eye salve! The city of Laodicea was noted for its eye salve, but the kind of medication the saints needed was not available in the apothecary shop. The eye is one of the body's most sensitive areas, and only the Great Physician can "operate" on it and make it what it ought to be. As He did with the man whose account is told in John 9, He might even irritate before He illuminates! But we must submit to His treatment, and then maintain good spiritual "health habits" so that our vision grows keener.

THEY HAD LOST THEIR VESTURE (3:17-18). Like the emperor in Hans Christian Andersen's story, these Christians thought they were clothed in splendor when they were really naked! To be naked meant to be defeated and humiliated (2 Sam. 10:4; Isa. 20:1-4). The Laodiceans could go to the market and purchase fine woolen garments, but that would not meet their real need. They needed the white garments of God's righteousness and grace. According to Revelation 19:8, we should be clothed in "fine linen, clean and white," and this symbolizes "the righteous acts of the saints" (NASB). Salvation means that Christ's righteousness is *imputed* to us, put to our account; but sanctification means that His righteousness is *imparted* to us, made a part of our character and conduct.

There is no divine commendation given to this church. Of course, the Laodiceans were busy commending themselves! They thought they were glorifying God, when in reality they were disgracing His name just as though they had been walking around naked.

The Lord closed this letter with three special statements:

First, *an explanation:* "As many as I love, I rebuke and chasten" (v. 19a). He still loved these lukewarm saints, even though their love for Him had grown cold. He planned to chasten them as proof of His love (Prov. 3:11-12; Heb. 12: 5-6). God permits churches to go through times of trial so that they might become what He wants them to become.

Second, *an exhortation:* "Be zealous therefore, and repent" (Rev. 3:19b). The church at Laodicea had to repent of their pride and humble themselves before the Lord. They had to "stir up that inner fire" (2 Tim. 1:6, PH) and cultivate a burning heart.

Finally, *an invitation* (Rev. 3:20-22). We often use these

verses to lead lost people to Christ, but the basic application is to the believer. The Lord was outside the Laodicean church! He spoke to the individual—"if any man"—and not to the whole congregation. He appealed to a small remnant in Sardis (3:4-5), and now He appeals to the individual. God can do great things in a church, even through one dedicated individual.

Christ was not impatient. "I have taken my stand" is the sense of the verb. He "knocks" through circumstances and He calls through His Word. For what is He appealing? Fellowship and communion, the people's desire to abide in Him. The Laodiceans were an independent church that had need of nothing, but they were not abiding in Christ and drawing their power from Him. They had a "successful program" but it was not fruit that comes from abiding in Christ (John 15:1-8).

Note that when we invite Him in, the supper room becomes a throne room! It is through communion with Christ that we find victory and become overcomers indeed.

The letters to the seven churches are God's X rays, given to us so that we might examine our own lives and ministries. Judgment is going to come to this world, but it first begins at God's house (1 Peter 4:17). In these letters we find encouragement as well as rebuke.

May the Lord help us to hear what the Spirit is saying *today* to the church, and to the individuals in the churches!

4

Come,
Let Us Adore Him!

Revelation 4—5

True spiritual worship is perhaps one of the greatest needs
in our individual lives and in our churches. There is a constant emphasis today on witnessing for Christ and working
for Christ, but not enough is said about worshiping Him. To
worship means "to ascribe worth" (see Rev. 4:11; 5:12). It
means to use all that we are and have to praise God for all
that He is and does.

Heaven is a place of worship, and God's people shall worship Him throughout all eternity. Perhaps it would be good
for us to get in practice now! A study of Revelation 4—5 will
certainly help us better understand how to worship God and
give Him the glory that He deserves.

If Revelation 1:19 is God's inspired outline of this book,
then chapter 4 ushers us into the third division: "the things
which shall be hereafter." In fact, that is exactly what God
said to John when He summoned him to heaven! It would
appear that, in this experience, John illustrates what will
happen to God's people when the Church Age has run its
course: heaven will open; there will be a voice and the sound
of a trumpet; and the saints will be caught up to heaven
(1 Thes. 4:13-18; 1 Cor. 15:52). Then, God's judgment of the
earth can begin.

But before God pours out His wrath, He gives us a glimpse into glory and permits us to hear the worshiping creatures in heaven as they praise God. Two aspects of their worship are presented for our instruction and imitation.

They Worship the Creator (Rev. 4)

The key word in this chapter is *throne;* it is used fourteen times. In fact, this is a key word in the entire book, appearing forty-six times. No matter what may happen on earth, God is on His throne and is in complete control. Various teachers interpret Revelation in different ways, but all agree that John is emphasizing the glory and sovereignty of God. What an encouragement that would be to the suffering saints of John's day and of every age in history.

Using the throne as the focal point, we can easily understand the arrangement of this exciting chapter.

ON THE THRONE—ALMIGHTY GOD (4:2-3). This is God the Father, since the Son approaches the throne in Revelation 5:6, and the Spirit is pictured before the throne in 4:5. There is no possible way for human words to describe what God is like in His essence. John can only use comparisons. Jasper is a clear gem (see 21:11) and the sardine is red. The Lord is robed in light, according to Psalm 104:2 and 1 Timothy 6:16. Both the jasper and the sardius (sardine) were found in the breastplate of the high priest (Ex. 28:17-21).

AROUND THE THRONE—A RAINBOW (4:3b). This rainbow was a complete circle, not merely an arc, for in heaven all things are completed. The rainbow reminds us of God's covenant with Noah (Gen. 9:11-17), symbolic of His promise that He would never again destroy the earth with a flood. God's covenant, as we shall see, was not only with Noah, but with all of His creation.

Judgment is about to fall, but the rainbow reminds us that God is merciful, even when He judges (Hab. 3:2). Usually, a rainbow appears *after* the storm; but here, we see it *before* the storm.

AROUND THE THRONE—ELDERS AND LIVING CREATURES (4:3-4,

6-7). No doubt the rainbow was around the throne vertically, while these heavenly beings were around the throne horizontally. They are, as it were, the king's court.

Who are these twenty-four elders seated on thrones? It is unlikely that they are angels, because angels are not numbered (Heb. 12:22), crowned, or enthroned. Besides, in Revelation 7:11, the elders are distinguished from the angels (see also 5:8-11). The crowns they wear are the "victor's crowns" (the Greek word *stephanos;* see 2:10); and we have no evidence that angels receive rewards.

These elders probably symbolize the people of God in heaven, enthroned and rewarded. There were twenty-four courses of priests in the Old Testament temple (1 Chron. 24:3-5, 18; see also Luke 1:5-9). God's people are "kings and priests" (Rev. 1:6), reigning and serving with Christ. Note especially their praise (5:9-10). When Daniel (Dan. 7:9) saw the thrones set up (not "cast down" as in the *King James Version*), they were empty; but when John saw them, they had been filled. Since there were twelve tribes of Israel and twelve apostles, perhaps the number twenty-four symbolizes the completion of God's people.

The white robes and palm branches speak of victory (see Rev. 7:9). These are the "overcomers" who have conquered because of their faith in Christ (1 John 5:4-5).

Also around the throne, John saw four "living creatures" ("beasts" in the *King James Version*) who were nearer to God than the angels and the elders. They resemble the cherubim that the Prophet Ezekiel saw (Ezek. 1:4-14; 10:20-22), but their praise (Rev. 4:8) reminds us of the seraphim of Isaiah 6. I believe that these special creatures symbolize God's creation and are related to God's covenant with Noah (Gen. 9:8-17). The faces of the living creatures parallel God's statement in Genesis 9:10—His covenant is with Noah (the face of the man), the fowl (the face of the eagle), the cattle (the face of the calf), and the beasts of the earth (the face of the lion).

These creatures signify the wisdom of God ("full of eyes")

and proclaim the holiness of God. They are heavenly reminders that God has a covenant with His creation and that He rules His creation from His throne. The presence of the emerald rainbow further enhances this image, since the rainbow was given as the sign of the creation covenant. No matter what terrible judgments may fall on God's earth, He will be faithful to keep His Word. Men may curse Him during the judgments (Rev. 16:9, 11, 21), but nature will praise Him and magnify His holiness.

The cherubim described in Ezekiel 1 seem to have a part in the providential workings of God in the world, pictured by the "wheels within the wheels." God uses the forces of nature to accomplish His will (Ps. 148), and all nature praises and thanks Him.

Some students see in the four faces described (Rev. 4:7) an illustration of the fourfold picture of Christ given in the Gospel accounts. Matthew is the royal Gospel of the King, illustrated by the lion. Mark emphasizes the servant aspect of the Lord's ministry (the calf). Luke presents Christ as the compassionate Son of man. John magnifies the deity of Christ, the Son of God (the eagle).

Finally, the name used by these creatures, "Lord God Almighty" emphasizes the power of God. As mentioned in chapter 1, the name *Almighty* is used nine times in Revelation. The only other such usage in the New Testament is 2 Corinthians 6:18, but it is found at least thirty-one times in Job, a book that magnifies the power of God in nature.

OUT OF THE THRONE—STORM SIGNALS (4:5a). "And from the throne proceed flashes of lightning and sounds and peals of thunder" (NASB). These are indications of a coming storm and reminders of God's awesome power (see Ex. 19:16; 9:23, 28). These "storm signals" will be repeated during the time of judgment, always proceeding from the throne and temple of God (Rev. 8:5; 11:19; 16:18). God has indeed prepared His throne for judgment (Ps. 9:7; note also 77:18).

Our world does not like to think of God as a God of judgment. They prefer to look at the rainbow around the throne and ignore the lightning and thunder out of the throne. He certainly is a God of grace, but His grace reigns *through righteousness* (Rom. 5:21). This was made clear at the Cross where God manifested both His love for sinners and His wrath against sin.

BEFORE THE THRONE—LAMPS AND A SEA (4:5b-6a). The seven lamps connote completeness and symbolize the Holy Spirit of God (1:4; note also Ezek. 1:13). John also seems to suggest in Revelation that the "heavenly sanctuary" follows the pattern of the earthly tabernacle and temple. (See Heb. 9:23.) The parallels are as follows:

Earthly temple	Heavenly sanctuary
Holy of holies	The throne of God
Seven-branched candlestick	Seven lamps of fire before the throne
Bronze laver	Sea of glass
Cherubim over the mercy seat	Four living creatures around the throne
Priests	Elders (kings and priests)
Brazen altar	Altar (6:9-11)
Incense altar	Incense altar (8:3-5)
Ark of the covenant	Ark of the covenant (11:19)

There is no temple in heaven in a material sense. All of heaven is God's sanctuary for those who serve before His holy throne (7:15). However, John indicates in Revelation 15:5-8 that there is a special "sanctuary" of God (note also 11:19). In the eternal state, there will be no temple (21:22).

A pure crystal sea symbolizes God's holiness, and the mingled fire speaks of His holy judgment. The crystal "firmament" in Ezekiel's vision also comes to mind (Ezek. 1:22); it was the foundation for God's throne. We shall meet this "sea of glass" again in Revelation 15 where it is connected with Israel's victory over Egypt.

PRAISE TO THE THRONE (4:9-11). Whenever the living creatures glorified God, the elders would fall before the throne and praise Him. The Book of Revelation is filled with hymns of praise (4:8, 11; 5:9-13; 7:12-17; 11:15-18; 12:10-12; 15:3-4; 16:5-7; 18:2-8; 19:2-6). The emphasis on praise is significant when you remember that John wrote this book to encourage people who were going through suffering and persecution!

The theme of this hymn is *God the Creator*, while in Revelation 5 the elders praise *God the Redeemer*. The praise in chapter 4 is given to the Father on the throne, while in chapter 5 it is directed to the Son (the Lamb) before the throne. The closing hymn (5:13) is expressed to both, another proof of the deity of Jesus Christ.

If the twenty-four elders typify the people of God in heaven, then we must ask, "Why should God's people praise God the Creator?" If the heavens are declaring the glory of God, why shouldn't God's heavenly people join the chorus? (Ps. 19) Creation bears constant witness to the power, wisdom, and glory of God. Acknowledging the Creator is the first step toward trusting the Redeemer (see Acts 14:8-18; 17:22-31). "All things were created by Him [Christ] and for Him . . . and by Him all things consist [hold together]" (Col. 1:16-17).

But sinful man worships and serves the creature rather than the Creator, and this is idolatry (Rom. 1:25). Furthermore, sinful man has polluted and destroyed God's wonderful creation; and he is going to pay for it (see Rev. 11:18). Creation is for God's praise and pleasure, and man has no right to usurp that which rightfully belongs to God. Man plunged creation into sin, so that God's *good* creation (Gen. 1:31) is today a *groaning* creation (Rom. 8:22); but because of Christ's work on the cross, it will one day be delivered and become a *glorious* creation (8:18-24).

It is unfortunate that the church today often neglects to worship the God of Creation. The real answer to the ecological problem is not financial or legal, but spiritual. It is only when man acknowledges the Creator and begins to use creation to God's glory that the problems will be solved.

They Worship the Redeemer (Rev. 5)

The focus of attention now shifts to a seven-sealed scroll in the hand of God. The scroll could not be read because it was rolled up and sealed (like a Roman will) with seven seals. John could see writing on both sides of the scroll, which meant that nothing more could be added. What was written was completed and final.

The scroll represents Christ's "title deed" to all that the Father promised Him because of His sacrifice on the cross. "Ask of Me, and I shall give Thee the heathen [nations] for Thine inheritance, and the uttermost parts of the earth for Thy possession" (Ps. 2:8). Jesus Christ is the "heir of all things" (Heb. 1:2). He is our beloved "Kinsman-Redeemer" who was willing to give His life to set us free from bondage and to restore our lost inheritance. (See Lev. 25:23-46; Jer. 32:6-15; the Book of Ruth.)

As Christ removed the seals, various dramatic events took place. The seventh seal introduced the seven trumpet judgments (Rev. 8:1-2). Then, when the seventh trumpet had blown, the great day of God's wrath was announced, ushering in the "vial [bowl] judgments" that brought to a climax the wrath of God (11:15ff; 15:1). It is possible that the trumpet judgments were written on one side of the scroll and the bowl judgments on the other.

A title deed or will can be opened only by the appointed heir, and this is Jesus Christ. No one in all the universe could be found worthy enough to break the seals. No wonder John wept, for he realized that God's glorious redemption plan for mankind could never be completed until the scroll was opened. The redeemer had to be near of kin, willing to redeem, and able to redeem. Jesus Christ meets all of the qualifications. He became flesh, so He is our kinsman. He loves us and is willing to redeem; and He paid the price, so He is able to redeem.

Now we are able to enter into the worship experience described in the remainder of Revelation 5. And we'll discover four compelling reasons why we worship Jesus Christ.

BECAUSE OF WHO HE IS (5:5-7). Three unique titles are given to our Lord to describe who He is. First, He is *the Lion of the tribe of Judah.* The reference here is to Genesis 49:8-10, where Jacob prophetically gave the scepter to Judah and made it the tribe of the kings. (God never meant for Saul to establish a dynasty, because he came from the tribe of Benjamin. God *used him* to discipline Israel because the people asked for a king; then He *gave them* David from the tribe of Judah.)

The image of "the lion" speaks of dignity, sovereignty, courage, and victory. Jesus Christ is the only living Jew who can prove His kingship from the genealogical records. "Son of David" was a title often used when He was ministering on earth (see Matt. 1).

But He is also *the Root of David,* which means He brought David (and David's line) into existence. As far as His humanity is concerned, Jesus had His roots *in* David (Isa. 11:1, 10); but as far as His deity is concerned, Jesus is the root *of* David. This speaks, of course, of our Lord's eternality; He is indeed the "Ancient of Days." How the Messiah could both be David's Lord and David's son was a problem Jesus presented to the Pharisees, and they could not (or would not) answer Him (Matt. 22:41-46).

When John turned to see, he saw not a lion but *a lamb!* Jesus Christ is called "the Lamb" at least twenty-eight times in the Book of Revelation (the Greek word used means "a little pet lamb") and the emphasis is not hard to miss. God's wrath is "the wrath of the Lamb" (Rev. 6:16). Cleansing is by "the blood of the Lamb" (7:14). The church is "the bride of the Lamb" (19:7; 21:9).

The theme of "the Lamb" is an important one throughout Scripture, for it presents the person and work of Jesus Christ, the Redeemer. The Old Testament question, "Where is the lamb?" (Gen. 22:7) was answered by John the Baptist who cried, "Behold the Lamb of God, which taketh away the sin of the world" (John 1:29). The choirs of heaven sing, "Worthy is the Lamb!" (Rev. 5:12)

The description of the Lamb (v. 6), if produced literally by an artist, would provide a grotesque picture; but when understood symbolically, conveys spiritual truth. Since seven is the number of perfection, we have here perfect power (seven horns), perfect wisdom (seven eyes), and perfect presence (seven Spirits in all the earth). The theologians would call these qualities omnipotence, omniscience, and omnipresence; and all three are attributes of God. The Lamb is God the Son, Christ Jesus!

We worship Jesus Christ because of who He is. But there is a second reason why we worship Him.

BECAUSE OF WHERE HE IS (5:6). To begin with, Jesus is in heaven. He is not in the manger, in Jerusalem, on the cross, or in the tomb. He is ascended and exalted in heaven. What an encouragement this is to suffering Christians, to know that their Saviour has defeated every enemy and is now controlling events from glory! He too suffered, but God turned His suffering into glory.

But where is Christ in heaven? He is *in the midst.* The Lamb is the center of all that transpires in heaven. All creation centers in Him (the four living creatures), as do all of God's people (the elders). The angels around the throne encircle the Saviour and praise Him.

He is also *at the throne.* Some sentimental Christian poetry and hymnody dethrones our Saviour and emphasizes only His earthly life. These poems and songs glamorize "the gentle carpenter" or "the humble teacher," but they fail to exalt the risen Lord! We do not worship a babe in a manger or a corpse on a cross. We worship the living, reigning Lamb of God who is in the midst of all in heaven.

BECAUSE OF WHAT HE DOES (5:8-10). When the Lamb came and took the scroll (see Dan. 7:13-14), the weeping ended and the praising began. God's people and the representatives of God's creation joined their voices in a new song of praise. Note that praise *and prayer* were united, for incense is a picture of prayer rising to the throne of God (Ps. 141:2; Luke 1:10). We shall meet the "incense prayers" of the saints again (Rev. 6:9-11; 8:1-6).

What kind of song did they sing? To begin with, it was *a worship hymn*, for they said, "Thou art worthy!" To *worship* means "to ascribe worth," and Jesus alone is worthy. When I was in the pastorate, I tried to open each morning worship service with a hymn that lifted the congregation's minds and hearts upward to the Lord Jesus Christ. Too many contemporary songs are "I" centered rather than "Christ" centered. They so emphasize the believer's experience that they almost ignore the Lord's glory. Certainly there is a place for that kind of song, but nothing can compare with adoring Christ in spiritual worship.

But this song was also *a Gospel song!* "Thou wast slain, and hast redeemed us [some texts read *them*] by Thy blood." The word translated *slain* means "violently slain" (see v. 6). Heaven sings about the Cross and the blood! I read about a denomination that revised its official hymnal and removed all songs about the blood of Christ. That hymnal could never be used in heaven, because there they glorify the Lamb slain for the sins of the world.

In Genesis 22, a ram was substituted for Isaac, a picture of Christ giving His life for *the individual*. (See Gal. 2:20.) At Passover, the lamb was slain for each *family* (Ex. 12:3). Isaiah states that Jesus died for *the nation of Israel* (Isa. 53:8; see also John 11:49-52). John affirms that the Lamb died for *the whole world!* (John 1:29) The more you meditate on the power and scope of Christ's work on the cross, the more humbled and worshipful you become.

This song was also *a missionary song*. Sinners were redeemed "out of every kindred, and tongue, and people, and nation" (Rev. 5:9). *Kindred* refers to a common ancestor and *tongue* to a common language. *People* means a common race, and *nation* a common rule or government. God loves a whole world (John 3:16) and His desire is that the message of redemption be taken to a whole world (Matt. 28:18-20).

Perhaps you heard about the Christian who was against foreign missions but somehow happened to attend a missionary rally. When they passed the offering plate, he told the usher, "I don't believe in missions!" "Then take something out," said the usher. "It's for the heathen."

This heavenly hymn was also *a devotional hymn,* for it announced our unique position in Christ as "a kingdom of priests." Like Melchizedek of old, believers are kings and priests (Gen. 14:17ff; Heb. 7; 1 Peter 2:5-10). The veil of the temple was torn when Jesus died, and the way is opened to God (Heb. 10:19-25). We "reign in life" as we yield to Christ and allow His Spirit to work in us (Rom. 5:17).

Finally, this song was *a prophetic hymn:* "We shall reign on the earth" (Rev. 5:10). When Jesus Christ returns to earth, He will establish His righteous kingdom for 1,000 years; and we shall reign with Him (20:1-6). The prayers of the saints, "Thy kingdom come!" will then be fulfilled. Creation shall then be set free from bondage to sin (Rom. 8:17-23; Isa. 11:1-10), and Christ shall reign in justice and power.

What a marvelous hymn! How rich would be our worship if only we would blend all these truths in honoring Him!

BECAUSE OF WHAT HE HAS (Rev. 5:11-14). In this closing burst of praise, all the angels and every creature in the universe joined together to worship the Redeemer. What a cascade of harmony John heard! In this hymn, they stated those things that Jesus Christ deserved to receive because of His sacrificial death on the cross. When He was on earth, people did not ascribe these things to Him; for many of these things He deliberately laid aside in His humiliation.

He was born in weakness and He died in weakness; but He is the recipient of all power. He became the poorest of the poor (2 Cor. 8:9), and yet He owns all the riches of heaven and earth. Men laughed at Him and called Him a fool; yet He is the very wisdom of God (1 Cor. 1:24; Col. 2:3).

He shared in the sinless weaknesses of humanity as He hungered, thirsted, and became weary. Today in glory, He possesses all strength. On earth, He experienced humiliation and shame as sinners ridiculed and reviled Him. They laughed at His kingship and attired Him in a mock robe, crown, and scepter. But all of that is changed now! He has received all honor and glory!

And blessing! He became a curse for us on the cross (Gal. 3:13), so that we can never be under the curse of the broken Law. (Some translations read "praise" instead of "blessing," but the Greek word carries both meanings.) He is worthy of all praise!

The worship service climaxed with all of the universe praising the Lamb of God and the Father seated on the throne!

And there was even a loud "Amen!" from the four living creatures! In heaven, we are permitted to say "Amen!"

Keep in mind that all of this praise centered on the Lord Jesus Christ, the Redeemer. It is not Christ the Teacher, but Christ the Saviour, who is the theme of their worship. While an unconverted person could praise the Creator, he certainly could not sincerely praise the Redeemer.

All of heaven's praise came because the Lamb took the scroll from the Father's hand. God's great eternal plan would now be fulfilled and creation would be set free from the bondage of sin and death. One day the Lamb will break the seals and put in motion events that will eventually lead to His coming to earth and the establishment of His kingdom.

As you share in these heavenly worship services, do you find your own heart saying "Amen!" to what they have sung? You may believe in Christ as the Creator, but have you trusted Him as your Redeemer?

If not, will you do so right now?

"Behold, I stand at the door and knock: if any man hear My voice, and open the door, I will come in to him, and will sup with him, and he with Me" (Rev. 3:20).

5

The Seals and the Sealed

Revelation 6—7

The worship described in Revelation 4—5 is preparation for the wrath described in Revelation 6—19. It seems strange to us that worship and judgment should go together, but this is because we do not fully understand either the holiness of God or the sinfulness of man. Nor do we grasp the total picture of what God wants to accomplish and how the forces of evil have opposed Him. God is long-suffering, but eventually He must judge sin and vindicate His servants.

According to Daniel 9:27, seven years are assigned to Israel in God's prophetic calendar, beginning with the signing of an agreement with the world dictator (the Antichrist), and ending with Christ's return to earth to judge evil and establish His kingdom. It is this period that is described in Revelation 6—19. By referring to John's outline (Rev. 1), you will see that his description is in three parts: the first three and a half years (chs. 6—9), the events at the middle of the period (chs. 10—14), and the last three and a half years (chs. 15—19).

What is so significant about the middle of the Tribulation? That is when the Antichrist breaks his covenant with Israel and becomes their persecutor instead of their protector (Dan. 9:27).

As you study these fourteen action-filled chapters, keep in mind that John wrote to encourage God's people in every age of history. He was not only writing *prophecy* that would be fulfilled in the end times; but he was also writing great *theology* and dramatically revealing the character of God and the principles of His kingdom. These chapters describe the cosmic conflict between God and Satan, the New Jerusalem and Babylon; and no matter what "key" a student may use to unlock Revelation, he cannot help but see the exalted King of kings as He vindicates His people and gives victory to His overcomers.

Since the church never knows when Christ will return, each generation must live in expectancy of His coming. Therefore the Book of Revelation must be able to communicate truth to each generation, not just to the people who will be alive when these events occur. Verses like 13:9, 16:15, and 22:7, 18-20 all indicate the timelessness of John's message. This also explains why the apostle used so much symbolism, for symbols never lose their meaning. In every era of its history, the church has had to contend with Babylon (compare Rev. 18:4 with Jer. 50—51) and Antichrist (see 1 John 2:18ff). Revelation 6—19 is merely the climax of this conflict.

In Revelation 6—7, John characterized the opening days of the Tribulation as a time of retribution, response, and redemption.

Retribution (Rev. 6:1-8)

In this section, John recorded the opening of the first four seals; and as each seal was opened, one of the four living creatures summoned a rider on a horse. ("Come and see" should read, "Come!") In other words, events take place on earth because of the sovereign direction of God in heaven.

The horse imagery is probably related to the vision described in Zechariah 1:7-17. Horses represent God's activity on earth, the forces He uses to accomplish His divine purposes. The center of His program is Israel, particularly the city of Jerusalem. (Jerusalem is mentioned thirty-nine times in Zechariah.) God has a covenant purpose for Israel, and that purpose will be fulfilled just as He promised.

Now, let's try to identify these horses and their riders.

ANTICHRIST (6:1-2). Daniel states that there is a "prince that shall come," who will make a covenant with Israel to protect her from her enemies (Dan. 9:26-27). In other words, the future world dictator begins his career as a peacemaker! He will go from victory to victory and finally control the whole world.

Some have suggested that the rider on the white horse is actually a symbol of the "conquering Christ" who today is defeating the forces of evil in the world. They point to Revelation 19:11 as proof, but the only similarity is the presence of a white horse. If this rider is indeed Jesus Christ, it seems strange that He should be named *at the end of the book* and not at the beginning!

We would expect the Antichrist to resemble *the* Christ, because Antichrist is Satan's great imitation! Even the Jews (who ought to know the Scriptures) will be deceived by him (John 5:43; 2 Thes. 2:1-12). This great deceiver will come as a peaceful leader, holding a bow but no arrows! (Our Lord's weapon is a sword; Rev. 19:15.) Antichrist will solve the world's problems and be received as the Great Liberator.

The word for *crown* in verse 2 is *stephanos*, which means "the victor's crown." The crown that Jesus Christ wears is *diadema*, "the kingly crown" (19:12). Antichrist could never wear the diadem, because it belongs only to the Son of God.

Certainly, there is a sense in which Jesus Christ is conquering today, as He releases people from the bondage of sin and Satan (Col. 1:13; Acts 26:18). But this conquest began with His victory on the cross and certainly did not have to wait for the opening of a seal! We shall note later that the sequence of events in Revelation 6 closely parallels the sequence given by our Lord in His Olivet discourse; and the first item mentioned is the appearance of false Christs (Matt. 24:5).

WAR (6:3-4). Antichrist's conquest begins in peace, but

soon he exchanges the empty bow for a sword. The color red is often associated with terror and death: the red dragon (Rev. 12:3), the red beast (17:3). It is a picture of wanton bloodshed. War has been a part of man's experience since Cain killed Abel, so this image would speak to believers in every age, reminding them that God is ultimately in control, even though He is not responsible for the lawless deeds of men and nations.

FAMINE (6:5-6). The color black is often connected with famine (Jer. 14:1-2; Lam. 5:10). Famine and war go together. A shortage of food will always drive up prices and force the government to ration what is available. "To eat bread by weight" is a Jewish phrase indicating that food is scarce (Lev. 26:26). A penny (denarius) a day was a standard wage for laborers (Matt. 20:2), but, of course, it had much greater buying power than the common penny does today. A "measure" of wheat was about two pints, sufficient for the daily needs of one person. Ordinarily, a person could buy eight to twelve measures for a penny, and much more of barley, which was the cheaper grain.

However, during the Tribulation, a man will have to work all day just to secure food for himself! There will be nothing for his family! At the same time, the rich will be enjoying plenty of oil and wine. No wonder Antichrist will eventually be able to control the economy (Rev. 13:17) as he promises to feed the hungry masses.

DEATH (6:7-8). John saw two personages: Death riding a pale horse and Hades (the realm of the dead) following him. Christ has the keys of death and hades (1:18), and both will one day be cast into hell (20:14). Death claims the body while hades claims the soul of the dead (20:13). John saw these enemies going forth to claim their prey, armed with weapons of the sword, hunger, pestilence (death), and wild beasts. In ancient times, hunger, pestilence, and the ravages of beasts would be expected to accompany war. (Note also Jer. 15:2; 24:10; Ezek. 14:21.)

Conquering tyrants who bring the world war, famine, and

pestilence are certainly nothing new. Suffering people from the days of the Roman Empire to the most recent war can easily recognize anticipations of these four dreaded horsemen. This is why the Book of Revelation has been a source of encouragement to suffering believers throughout history. As they see the Lamb opening the seals, they realize that God is in control and that His purposes will be accomplished.

Response (Rev. 6:9-17)

John recorded two responses to the opening of the seals, one in heaven and the other on earth.

THE MARTYRS (6:9-11). When the Old Testament priest presented an animal sacrifice, the victim's blood was poured out at the base of the brazen altar (Lev. 4:7, 18, 25, 30). In Old Testament imagery, blood represents life (17:11). So, here in Revelation, the souls of the martyrs "under the altar" indicates that their lives were given sacrificially to the glory of God. The Apostle Paul had the same idea in mind when he wrote Philippians 2:17 and 2 Timothy 4:6.

The Greek word *martus*, which gives us our English word *martyr* simply means "a witness." (See Rev. 2:13; 17:6.) These saints were slain by the enemy because of their witness to the truth of God and the message of Jesus Christ. The forces of Antichrist do not accept the truth, because Satan wants them to be deceived and accept his lies (see 19:20; 20:10; also 2 Thes. 2:9-12).

Since their murderers are still alive on earth, these martyrs are apparently from the early part of the Tribulation. But they represent *all* who have laid down their lives for Jesus Christ and the cause of God's truth, and they are an encouragement to all today who may be called to follow them. They assure us that the souls of the martyrs are in heaven, awaiting the resurrection (Rev. 20:4), and that they are at rest, robed in heavenly glory.

But is it "Christian" for these martyred saints to pray for vengeance on their murderers? After all, both Jesus and Stephen prayed that God would forgive those who killed them.

I have no doubt that, when they were slain on earth, these martyrs also prayed for their slayers; and this is the right thing to do (Matt. 5:10-12, 43-48).

The great question, however, was not *whether* their enemies would be judged, but *when.* "How long, O Lord?" has been the cry of God's suffering people throughout the ages. (See Pss. 74:9-10; 79:5; 94:3-4; also Hab. 1:2.) The saints in heaven know that God will eventually judge sin and establish righteousness in the earth, but they do not know God's exact schedule. It is not personal revenge that they seek, but vindication of God's holiness and the establishment of God's justice. Every believer today who sincerely prays, "Thy kingdom come!" is echoing their petition.

God made clear to these martyrs that their sacrifice was an appointment, not an accident; and that others would join them. Even in the death of His people, God is in control (Ps. 116:15); so there is nothing to fear.

Many others would be slain for their faith before the Lord would return and establish His kingdom. (See Rev. 11:7; 12:11; 14:13; and 20:4-5.) Then as today, it appears that the enemy is winning; but God will have the last word. Even in our "enlightened" twentieth century, multiplied thousands of true believers have laid down their lives for Christ; certainly they will receive the crown of life (2:10).

THE EARTH-DWELLERS (6:12-17). The martyrs cried, "Avenge us!" but the unbelievers on earth will cry, "Hide us!" The opening of the sixth seal will produce worldwide convulsions and catastrophes, including the first of three great earthquakes (6:12; 11:13; 16:18-19). All of nature will be affected: the sun, moon, and stars, as well as the heavens, the mountains, and the islands. Compare this scene with Joel 2:30-31 and 3:15 as well as with Isaiah 13:9-10 and 34:2-4.

Even though John wrote using symbolic language, these verses describe a scene that would frighten even the most courageous person. People will try to hide from the face of God and from the face of the Lamb! Imagine wanting to hide from *a lamb!* I once heard Dr. Vance Havner say that the day would come when the most expensive piece of real estate would be a hole in the ground and he was right.

We will see more of "the wrath of God" as we progress through Revelation (11:18; 14:10; 16:19; 19:15). We will also encounter the wrath of Satan (12:17) and the wrath of the nations as they oppose God (11:18). If men and women will not yield to the love of God, and be changed by the grace of God, then there is no way for them to escape the wrath of God.

Rank and wealth will not deliver anyone in that terrible day. John's list included kings, captains, and slaves, the rich and the poor. "Who shall be able to stand?"

The phrase "wrath of the Lamb" seems a paradox. "Wrath of the lion" would be more consistent. We are so accustomed to emphasizing the meekness and gentleness of Christ (Matt. 11:28-30) that we forget His holiness and justice. The same Christ who welcomed the children in the temple also drove the merchants from that same temple. God's wrath is not like a child's temper tantrum or punishment meted out by an impatient parent. God's wrath is the evidence of His holy love for all that is right and His holy hatred for all that is evil. Only a soft and sentimental person would want to worship a God who did not deal justly with evil in the world.

Furthermore, the people mentioned here are *impenitent.* They refuse to submit to God's will. They would rather hide from God in fear (remember Adam and Eve?) than run to Him in faith. They are proof that judgment *by itself* does not change the human heart. Not only will men seek to hide from God, but they will blaspheme Him as well! (Rev. 16:9, 11, 21)

But is there any hope for believers during this terrible time of judgment? And what about God's special people, the Jews, who made a covenant with the Antichrist? Certainly people will trust the Lord even after the church is taken to heaven, but how will they manage? We turn to Revelation 7 for some of the answers.

But before considering John's third theme in this section—

redemption—we must note the parallels that exist between Christ's prophetic words recorded in Matthew 24 and what John wrote in Revelation 6. The following summary outline makes this clear.

Matthew 24	Revelation 6
False Christs (vv. 4-5)	White horse rider (vv. 1-2)
Wars (v. 6)	Red horse—war (vv. 3-4)
Famines (v. 7a)	Black horse—famine (vv. 5-6)
Death (vv. 7b-8)	Pale horse—death (vv. 7-8)
Martyrs (v. 9)	Martyrs under the altar (vv. 9-11)
Worldwide chaos (vv. 10-13)	Worldwide chaos (vv. 12-17)

Matthew (24:14) introduces the preaching of the Gospel of the kingdom throughout the whole world, and this may well be where Revelation 7 fits in. God may use the sealed 144,000 Jews to share His Word with the world, resulting in the salvation of multitudes.

Redemption (Rev. 7:1-17)
It is important that we contrast the two groups of people described in this chapter.

7:1-8	7:9-17
Jews	Gentiles from all nations
Numbered - 144,000	Not numbered, nor could be
Sealed on earth	Standing in heaven before God

While we are not told explicitly in Scripture that the 144,000 Jews are God's special witnesses, and that the Gentile host is saved through their ministry, this appears to be a logical deduction; otherwise, why are they associated in this chapter? The parallel with Matthew 24:14 also indicates that the 144,000 will witness for the Lord during the Tribulation.

THE SEALED JEWS (7:1-8). Angels are associated with the forces of nature: the wind (Rev. 7:1), fire (14:18), and water (16:5). Stopping the winds implies a "lull before the storm." God controls all of nature. During the day of His wrath, He will use the forces of nature to judge mankind. The phrase "four corners of the earth" is no more "unscientific" here than it is in Isaiah 11:12 or the daily newspaper.

In Scripture, a seal indicates ownership and protection. Today, God's people are sealed by the Holy Spirit (Eph. 1:13-14). This is God's guarantee that we are saved and safe, and that He will one day take us to heaven. The 144,000 Jews will receive the Father's name as their seal (Rev. 14:1), in contrast to the "mark of the beast" that Antichrist will give those who follow him (13:17; 14:11; 16:2; 19:20).

This seal will protect these chosen Jews from the judgments that will "hurt the earth and the sea" (7:2), and occur when the first four angels blow their trumpets (ch. 8). The judgments are intensified when the horrible locusts are released from the pit (9:1-4). Protected from these awesome judgments, the 144,000 will be able to do their work and glorify the Lord.

In every age, God has had His faithful remnant. Elijah thought he was alone, but God had 7,000 who were yet faithful to Him (1 Kings 19:18). The sealing described in Revelation 7 certainly has its background in Ezekiel 9:1-7, where the faithful were sealed before God's judgment fell. So, while these 144,000 Jews are an elect people in the last days with a special task from God, they also symbolize God's faithful elect in every age of history.

The number 144,000 is significant because it signifies perfection and completeness (144 = 12 x 12). Some see here the completeness of *all* God's people: the twelve tribes of Israel (Old Testament saints) and the twelve apostles (New Testament saints). This may be a good *application* of this passage, but it is not the basic *interpretation*; for we are told that these 144,000 are all Jews, and even their tribes are named.

A man once told me he was one of the 144,000; so I asked him, "To which tribe do you belong, and can you prove it?" Of course, he could not prove it, no more than a Jew today can prove the tribe from which he or she descended. The genealogical records have all been destroyed. Even the fact that ten of the tribes were taken by the Assyrians and "lost" is no problem to God. He knows His people and their whereabouts (see Matt. 19:28; Acts 26:7; James 1:1).

This is not to say that our literal interpretation of this passage is not without problems. Why is Levi included when it had no inheritance with the other tribes? (Num. 18:20-24; Josh. 13:14) Why is Joseph named but not his son Ephraim, who is usually connected with his brother Manasseh? Finally, why is the tribe of Dan omitted here and yet included in Ezekiel's list for the apportionment of the land? (Ezek. 48:1) Many suggestions have been made, but we do not know the answers. Even if we interpreted this passage in a spiritual sense (i.e., Israel is the church), we would be no more certain. We must permit God to know "the secret things," and not allow our ignorance of them to hinder us from obeying what we *do* know (Deut. 29:29).

THE SAVED GENTILES (7:9-17). You cannot read the Book of Revelation without developing a global outlook, for the emphasis is on what God does for people in the *whole* world. The Lamb died to redeem people "out of every kindred, and tongue, and people, and nation" (Rev. 5:9). The great multitudes pictured here came from "all nations, and kindreds, and people, and tongues" (7:9). "Go ye into all the world, and preach the Gospel to every creature" was our Lord's mandate (Mark 16:15).

There is no doubt as to who this multitude is, because one of the elders explained it to John (v. 14): they are Gentiles who have been saved through faith in Christ during the Tribulation. (We will meet this same group again in Revelation 14.) While today, in most parts of the world, it is relatively easy to confess Christ, this will not be the case during the Tribulation, at least during the last half of it. Then, unless persons wear the "mark of the beast," they will not be able to buy or sell; and this would leave them without even life's bare necessities. Verse 16 indicates that they suffered hunger (see 13:17), thirst (see 16:4), and lack of shelter. (On the heat of the sun, see 16:8-9.)

The fact that they are *standing* before the throne and not seated around it indicates that these people are not identified with the twenty-four elders. In fact, John himself did not know who they were! If they had been Old Testament believers, or the church, John would have recognized them. That the elder had to tell John who they were suggests that they are a special people, which, indeed, they are.

Of course, in the heavenly city (Rev. 21—22), all distinctions will cease and we shall all simply be the people of God in glory. But while God is working out His program in human history, distinctions still exist between the Jews, the Gentiles, the church, and the Tribulation saints.

John gave a beautiful description of these people.

First, they were *accepted*, for they stood before God's throne and the Lamb. No doubt they had been rejected on earth for they stood for truth at a time when lies were popular and Satan was in charge. Their white robes and palms symbolize victory: they were true overcomers! The Jews used palm branches at their Feast of Tabernacles (Lev. 23:40-43), which was a special time of national rejoicing.

Then, they were *joyful*. They sang praises to the Father and to the Lamb; and their worship was joined by all those who surrounded the throne.

Third, they were *rewarded*. They had the privilege of being before God's throne and of serving Him. When God's people get to heaven, there will be work to do! We shall be able to serve Him perfectly! The Lamb will shepherd us and satisfy us with every good thing (see Isa. 49:10; Rev. 21:4).

The opening of the seventh seal will introduce the seven "trumpet judgments" (Rev. 8—11) and the wrath of God will increase both in intensity and scope. But before that occurs, we are assured that in His wrath, God will remember mercy (Hab. 3:2). Despite the wrath of God and the terror inspired by Satan and his helpers, multitudes will be saved through the blood of Jesus Christ. No matter what the age or dispensation, God's way of salvation has always been the same: faith in Jesus Christ, the Lamb of God.

Sad to say, however, multitudes during that time will also reject the Saviour and trust "the beast." But are there not people *today* who prefer Satan to Christ and this world to the world to come? They are just as condemned as the Tribulation sinners who receive the "mark of the beast."

If you have never trusted the Saviour, do so now.

If you have trusted Him, then share the Good News of salvation with others that they might be delivered from the wrath to come.

6

Blow the Trumpets!

Revelation 8—9

The seal judgments now over, the trumpet judgments are about to begin. These will be followed by the bowl (vial) judgments, culminating in the destruction of Babylon and Christ's return to earth. Note that from the seals to the trumpets to the bowls, the judgments increase in their intensity. Note also that the trumpet and the bowl judgments touch on the same areas, as the following summary illustrates:

The Trumpets	The Judgment	The Bowls
1. 8:1-7	The earth	16:1-2
2. 8:8-9	The sea	16:3
3. 8:10-11	The rivers	16:4-7
4. 8:12-13	The heavens	16:8-9
5. 9:1-2	Mankind—torment	16:10-11
6. 9:13-21	An army	16:12-16
7. 11:15-19	Angry nations	16:17-21

The trumpet judgments are released during the first half of the Tribulation, and the bowl judgments during the last half, which is also called "the wrath of God" (Rev. 14:10; 15:7). The trumpet judgments parallel the plagues that God sent upon the land of Egypt. And why not? After all, the whole world will be saying, as did Pharaoh, "Who is the Lord that we should serve Him?"

The opening of the seventh seal, and the blowing of the first six trumpets, brought about three dramatic results.

Preparation (Rev. 8:1-6)

This preparation involves two factors: silence (8:1) and supplication (8:2-6).

The hosts in heaven had just worshiped the Father and the Lamb with a tremendous volume of praise (7:10-12). But when the Lamb opened the seventh seal, heaven was silent for about thirty minutes. John does not tell us what caused the silence, but several possibilities exist. The scroll had now been opened completely, and perhaps even turned over; and all of heaven could see God's glorious plan unfolding. Perhaps the heavenly hosts were simply awestruck at what they saw.

Certainly, this silence was "the lull before the storm," for God's intensified judgments were about to be hurled to the earth. "Hold thy peace at the presence of the Lord God: for the day of the Lord is at hand" (Zeph. 1:7; note also vv. 14-18, especially v. 16, "A day of the trumpet"). "Be silent, O all flesh, before the Lord: for He is raised up out of His holy habitation" (Zech. 2:13). "The Lord is in His holy temple: let all the earth keep silence before Him" (Hab. 2:20).

During this silence, the seven angels were given trumpets, significant to John, because he was a Jew and understood the place of trumpets in Israel's national life. According to Numbers 10, trumpets had three important uses: they called the people together (vv. 1-8); they announced war (v. 9); and they announced special times (v. 10). The trumpet sounded at Mount Sinai when the Law was given (Ex. 19:16-19), and trumpets were blown when the king was anointed and enthroned (1 Kings 1:34, 39). Of course, everyone familiar with the Old Testament would remember the trumpets at the conquest of Jericho (Josh. 6:13-16).

The voice of the Lord Jesus Christ sounded to John like a trumpet (Rev. 1:10). The voice of a trumpet summoned John to heaven (4:1), and some relate this to the promise of the rapture of the church given in 1 Thessalonians 4:13-18. Sounding seven trumpets certainly would announce a declaration of war, as well as the fact that God's anointed King was enthroned in glory and about to judge His enemies (Ps. 2:1-5). As trumpets declared defeat to Jericho, they will ultimately bring defeat to Babylon.

The awesome silence was followed by the actions of a special angel at the golden altar in heaven (see Rev. 9:13; 14:18; 16:7). In the tabernacle and temple, the golden altar stood before the veil and was used for burning incense (Ex. 30:1-10). This was the ministry Zacharias was performing when the angel told him that he and Elisabeth would have a son (Luke 1:5ff). Burning incense on this altar was a picture of prayer ascending to God (Ps. 141:2).

The "prayers of the saints" (Rev. 8:4) are not the prayers of a special group of people in heaven who have arrived at "sainthood." To begin with, *all* God's children are saints—set apart for God—through faith in Jesus Christ (2 Cor. 1:1; 9:1, 12; 13:13). And there is no definite teaching in the Scriptures that people in heaven pray for believers on earth, or that we can direct our prayers to God through them. We pray to the Father through the Son, for He alone is worthy (Rev. 5:3). For centuries, God's people have been praying, "Thy kingdom come, Thy will be done!" and now those prayers are about to be answered. Likewise, the Tribulation martyrs prayed for God to vindicate them (6:9-11), a common plea of David in the Psalms (see Pss. 7, 26, 35, 52, 55, and 58 for example). These "imprecatory psalms" are not expressions of selfish personal vengeance, but rather cries for God to uphold His holy Law and vindicate His people.

On the great Day of Atonement, the high priest would put incense on the coals in the censer and, with the blood of the sacrifice, enter the holy of holies (Lev. 16:11-14). But in this scene, the angel put the incense on the altar (presented the prayers before God) and then *cast the coals* from the altar to the earth! The parallel in Ezekiel 10 indicates that this symbolized God's judgment; and the effects described in Revelation 8:5 substantiate this view. A storm is about to begin! (See 4:5; 11:19; 16:18.)

Like it or not, the prayers of God's people are involved in the judgments that He sends. The throne and the altar are related. The purpose of prayer, it has often been said, is not to get man's will done in heaven, but to get God's will done on earth—even if that will involves judgment. True prayer is serious business, so we had better not move the altar too far from the throne!

Desolation (Rev. 8:7-13)

The first four trumpet judgments are "natural" in that they affect the land, the saltwater, the fresh water, and the heavenly bodies. The fifth and sixth judgments involve the release of demonic forces that first torment, and then kill. The last of the trumpet judgments (11:15-19) creates a crisis among all the nations of the world.

DESOLATION ON EARTH (8:7). "Hail and fire mingled with blood" reminds us of the seventh plague that God sent against Egypt (Ex. 9:18-26). The Prophet Joel also promised "blood and fire" in the last days (Joel 2:30). Since this is a supernatural judgment, it is not necessary to try to explain how hail, fire, and blood become mingled. "Fire" could refer to the lightning of a severe electrical storm.

The target for this judgment is green vegetation, the trees and the grass, one-third of which is burned up. One can well imagine how this would affect not only the balance of nature, but also the food supply. The Greek word for *trees* usually means "fruit trees"; and the destruction of pasture lands would devastate the meat and milk industries.

DESOLATION IN THE SEAS (8:8-9). Turning water into blood reminds us of the first Egyptian plague (Ex. 7:19-21). Note that John did not say that an actual burning mountain was cast out of heaven, but that the fiery object was like a great mountain. A triple judgment resulted: a third part of the saltwater turned to blood, a third part of the marine life died, and a third of the ships were destroyed. This will be an ecological and an economic disaster of unprecedented proportions.

Considering that the oceans occupy about three-fourths of the earth's surface, you can imagine the extent of this judgment. The pollution of the water and the death of so many creatures would greatly affect the balance of life in the oceans, and this would undoubtedly lead to further insoluable problems. As of January 1, 1981, there were 24,867 ocean-going merchant ships registered. Imagine the shock waves that would hit the shipping industry if 8,289 valuable ships were suddenly destroyed! And what about their cargoes!

Some interpreters take "the sea" to mean the Mediterranean Sea. However, this would make a relatively small impact on the world, since the Mediterranean covers only 969,100 square miles and averages just 5,000 feet deep. It is likely that all the major bodies of saltwater are included in this judgment.

DESOLATION IN THE FRESH WATER (8:10-11). God's wrath next reaches *inland* and touches the rivers and fountains of water (wells and sources of the rivers), making the fresh water taste bitter like wormwood. The National Geographic Society lists about 100 principal rivers in the world, ranging in length from the Amazon (4,000 miles long) to the Rio de la Plata (150 miles long). The U.S. Geological Survey reports thirty large rivers in the United States, beginning with the mighty Mississippi (3,710 miles long). One-third of these rivers, and their sources, will become so bitterly polluted that drinking their water could produce death.

God has His stars numbered and named (Job 9:9-10). It is likely that this fallen star is molten and that, as it nears the earth, it begins to disintegrate and fall into the various bodies of water. If a star actually struck the earth, our globe would be destroyed; so this star must "come apart" as it enters the atmosphere. Of course, this event is a divinely-controlled judgment; therefore, we must not try to limit it by the known laws of science.

The word translated *wormwood* gives us our English word *absinthe*, which is a popular liqueur in some countries of the world. The word means "undrinkable," and in the Old Testament was synonymous with sorrow and great calamity. Jeremiah, "the Weeping Prophet," often used it (Jer. 9:15; 23:15; Lam. 3:15, 19), and so did Amos (Amos 5:7; "those who turn justice into wormwood," NASB). Moses warned that idolatry would bring sorrow to Israel, like a root producing wormwood (Deut. 29:18). Solomon warned that immorality might seem pleasant, but in the end, it produces bitterness like wormwood (Prov. 5:4).

If the people who *drink from* these waters are in danger of dying, what must happen to the fish and other creatures that *live in* these waters? And what would happen to the vegetation near these rivers? If the ecologists are worried about the deadly consequences of water pollution today, what will they think when the third trumpet blows?

There is no direct parallel here to any of the plagues of Egypt. However, after the Exodus, Israel encountered bitter waters at Marah (which means "bitter") and Moses had to purify the water supply (Ex. 15:23-27). But no supernatural purification will be available during the Tribulation.

DESOLATION IN THE HEAVENS (8:12-13). The judgments from the first three trumpets affected only a third part of the land and waters, but this fourth judgment affects the entire world. Why? Because it gets to the very source of the earth's life and energy, the sun. With one-third less sunlight on the earth, there will be one-third less energy available to support the life systems of man and nature.

This judgment parallels the ninth plague in Egypt (Ex. 10:21-23), which lasted three days. "The day of the Lord is darkness, and not light" (Amos 5:18). Think of the vast changes in temperatures that will occur and how these will affect human health and food growth.

It is possible that this particular judgment is temporary, for the fourth bowl judgment will reverse it, and the sun's power will be intensified (Rev. 16:8-9). Then, at the close of the Tribulation, the sun and moon will be darkened again to announce the Saviour's return (Matt. 24:29-30; see also Luke 21:25-28).

"Blow ye the trumpet in Zion," said the Prophet Joel, "for the day of the Lord cometh . . . a day of darkness and of gloominess" (Joel 2:1-2). Darkness, indeed! Not only will nature suffer loss, but human nature will take advantage of the long darkness and no doubt indulge in crime and wickedness. "Every one that doeth evil hateth the light" (John 3:20).

At this point, a remarkable messenger will appear in the sky, proclaiming woe to the earth's inhabitants. Most manuscripts have "eagle" here instead of "angel," but either one would certainly get people's attention! Could this be the eaglelike living creature that John saw worshiping before the throne? (Rev. 4:7-8) Will God send it on this special mission? We cannot say for sure, but it is a possibility.

The three "woes" in verse 13 refer to the judgments yet to come when the remaining three angels blow their trumpets. It is as though the messenger cried, "If you think this has been terrible, just wait! The worst is yet to come!"

The phrase "inhabiters of the earth" (or "them that dwell on the earth") is found twelve times in Revelation (3:10; 6:10; 8:13; 11:10; 12:12; 13:8, 12, 14; 14:6; 17:2, 8). It means much more than "people who live on the earth," for that is where *all* living people reside. Instead, it refers to a *kind* of people: those who live *for* the earth and the things *of* the earth. These are just the opposite of people who have their citizenship in heaven (Phil. 3:18-21). John described this worldly sort well in his first epistle (1 John 2:15-17), and later in this prophecy he again makes it clear that "earth-dwellers" are not born again (Rev. 13:8).

At the beginning of human history, heaven and earth were united because our first parents honored God and obeyed His will. Satan tempted them to focus on the earth; they disobeyed God; and ever since, a great gulf has been fixed between heaven and earth. This chasm was bridged when the Son of God came to earth and died for the sins of the world.

Liberation (Rev. 9:1-21)

The late Dr. Wilbur M. Smith, who made the Book of Revelation his special study, once wrote: "It is probable that, apart from the exact identification of Babylon in chapters 17 and 18, the meaning of the two judgments in this chapter represents the most difficult major problem in the Revelation" (*Wycliffe Bible Commentary*, p. 1509). Revelation 9 describes two frightening armies that are liberated at just the right time and permitted to judge mankind.

THE ARMY FROM THE PIT (9:1-12). The "bottomless pit" is literally "the pit of the abyss." Luke makes it clear that this "pit" is the abode of the demons (Luke 8:31), and John states that Satan will be temporarily "jailed" there during our Lord's reign on the earth (Rev. 20:1-3). The Antichrist (i.e., "the beast") will ascend out of this pit (11:7; 17:8). It is not the lake of fire, for that is the final "prison" for Satan and all who follow him (20:10), but part of that hidden underworld under the Lord's authority. Today, the fearsome army described here is already incarcerated, waiting for the hour of liberation.

This fallen star is a person, the king over the beings in the pit (v. 11). He does not have *complete* authority, for the key to the pit had to be given to him before he could loose his army. This "star" is probably Satan and the army, his demons (Eph. 6:10ff). One of the names for Satan is *Lucifer*, which means "brightness"; he also is compared to the "morning star" (Isa. 14:12-14). Jesus said to His disciples, "I beheld Satan as lightning fall from heaven" (Luke 10:18).

When the pit was opened, smoke emerged as though the door of a furnace had been loosened. Jesus compared hell to a furnace of fire (Matt. 13:42, 50), an image that ought to make people stop and think before they jest about it. The smoke polluted the air and darkened the sun, which had already been darkened when the fourth trumpet sounded.

But it is what came out of the smoke that truly terrorized mankind: an army of demons, compared to locusts. The eighth plague in Egypt was a devastating swarm of locusts (Ex. 10:1-20). People who have never encountered these insects have little idea of the damage they can do. When God wanted to judge His people, He would sometimes send locusts to devour the harvests (Deut. 28:38, 42; Joel 2).

These are not literal locusts, because locusts do not have scorpionlike stings in their tails. These creatures do not devour the green vegetation; in fact, they are prohibited from doing so. This demonic army is given the assignment of tormenting all who have not been protected by the seal of God. The 144,000 men from the tribes of Israel would therefore escape this painful judgment (Rev. 7:1-8). In fact, it is likely that *all* who have trusted the Lord will be sealed in some special way and protected from torment.

The normal lifespan of the locust is about five months (May to September), and this is the length of time that the judgment will last. These demons will sting people and thus create such pain that their victims will actually want to die, but death will flee from them (Jer. 8:3).

Reading the detailed description of these creatures, we realize that John is not writing about ordinary locusts. Yet, despite its obvious symbolism, it aptly portrays a powerful enemy armed for battle. With bodies like horses but faces like men, the demons' heads are crowned and covered with long hair. They have teeth like those of lions, and their skin is like a coat of mail. When they fly, the noise is like an army of chariots rushing by. It is unnecessary to try to "spiritualize" these symbols, or to interpret them in light of modern means of warfare. John is heaping image upon image to force us to feel the horror of this judgment.

Real locusts do not have a king (Prov. 30:27), but this army follows the rule of Satan, the angel of the bottomless pit. His name is "Destroyer." "The thief [Satan] cometh not, but for to steal, and to kill, and to destroy" (John 10:10). Real locusts are pervasive destroyers, but this army only tortures those who do not belong to the Lord.

As God's people, we can be thankful that Jesus Christ holds the keys of hell and death (Rev. 1:18) and exercises divine authority even over Satan. God has His timetable for all these events, and nothing will happen too soon or too late (2 Thes. 2:6; note also Rev. 9:15).

THE ARMY FROM THE EAST (9:13-21). It was at the golden altar of incense that the angel offered the prayers of the saints (8:3-5); now from this same altar a voice speaks, commanding that four angels be loosed. These angels are apparently wicked, because no holy angel would be bound. Each angel is in charge of part of the vast army that follows them at their liberation, an army of 200 million beings! The army is released at a precise time, for a special purpose: to kill (not just torment) a third of the world's population. Since a fourth of mankind has already been killed (6:8), this means that *half of the world's population will be dead* by the time the sixth trumpet judgment is completed.

Are we to identify this as a literal army of men, moving in conquest across the globe? Probably not. For one thing, the emphasis in this paragraph is not on the riders, but on the horses. The description cannot fit war-horses as we know them, or, for that matter, modern warfare equipment, such as tanks. To assert that this is a literal army, and to point to some nation (such as China) that claims to have 200 million soldiers, is to miss the message John is seeking to convey.

The deadly power of these horses is in their mouths and tails, not in their legs. Fire, smoke, and brimstone issue from their mouths, and their tails are like biting serpents. They can attack men from the front as well as from the rear.

I take it that this is another demonic army, headed by four fallen angels; and that all of them are today bound by the Lord, unable to act until God gives them permission. Why they are bound at the Euphrates River is not explained, though that area is the cradle of civilization (Gen. 2:14), not to mention one of the boundaries for Israel (15:18).

One would think that the combination of five months of torment and then death (from fire, smoke, and brimstone) would bring men and women to their knees in repentance; but such is not the case. These judgments are not remedial but retributive: God is upholding His holy law and vindicating His suffering people (see Rev. 6:9-11). Even a casual reading of verses 20-21 reveals the awful wickedness of mankind, even in the midst of God's judgments. The most frightening thing about Revelation 9 is not the judgments that God sends but the sins that men persist in committing *even while God is judging them.*

Consider the sins that men and women will be committing:

Demon worship, which goes hand-in-hand with *idolatry* (see 1 Cor. 10:19-21), will be the leading sin. Satan will be at work (always under the permissive will of God), and Satan has always wanted to be worshiped (Isa. 14:12-15; Matt. 4:8-10). A great deal of "religion" will be practiced at this time, but it will be false religion. People will worship the works of their own hands, which could well include the buildings they construct, the machines they make, and the cities they build, as well as their idols.

Here are dead sinners worshiping dead gods! (See Ps. 115.) Their gods will not be able to protect or deliver them, yet these people will continue to reject the true God and worship Satan and idols!

Murder and *theft* will also be rife in those days. So will various kinds of *sexual immorality.* The word translated *sorcery* is the Greek word *pharmakia*, which means "the use of drugs." Drugs are often used in pagan religious rites and demon worship. As we see the expansion of today's "drug culture," we have no problem envisioning a whole society given over to these demonic practices.

Mankind will be breaking the first two Mosaic commandments by making and worshiping idols. In their murders, they will violate the sixth commandment, and in their thefts, the eighth. By their fornication, they will break the seventh commandment. It will be an age of lawlessness with "every man doing that which is right in his own eyes" (see Jud. 21:25).

But God is working out His plan; and neither the sins of mankind nor the schemes of Satan will hinder Him from accomplishing His will.

We have come now to the midpoint of the Tribulation (Rev. 10—14), a time during which some important events must take place. Thus far, we have covered about three and a half years of this seven-year period (Dan. 9:27). During this time, Antichrist began his career as a peacemaker and a special friend to Israel; but now, his true character will be revealed. He will become a peace-breaker and a persecutor of the people of God.

Things will not look bright for God's people during this middle stage of the prophetic journey, but they will still be overcomers through the power of the King of kings and Lord of lords!

7

A Time for Testimony

Revelation 10—11

Revelation 10—14 describes the events that will occur at the middle of the seven-year Tribulation. This explains John's repeated mention of the three-and-a-half-year time segment in one form or another (11:2-3; 12:6, 14; 13:5). At the beginning of this period, the Antichrist began to make his conquest by promising to protect the Jews and assist in their rebuilding of the temple in Jerusalem. But after three and a half years, he will break his agreement, invade the temple, and begin to persecute the Jewish people.

However depressing the events of this middle segment of the Tribulation may be, God is not without His witness to the world. In Revelation 10—11 are three important testimonies: from a mighty angel (10:1-11), from the two special witnesses (11:1-14), and from the elders in heaven (11:15-19).

The Testimony of the Mighty Angel (Rev. 10:1-11)

More than sixty references to angels are made in Revelation. After all, they are God's army sent to accomplish His purposes on earth. Believers today seldom think about the ministry of these servants (Heb. 1:14), but one day in heaven we shall learn about all they did for us here.

THE DESCRIPTION OF THE ANGEL (10:1-4) amazes us, for he has some of the characteristics that belong especially to the Lord Jesus Christ. John had seen and heard a "strong angel" (Rev. 5:2), and the same Greek word is here translated *mighty*. All angels excel in strength (Ps. 103:20), but apparently some have greater power and authority than others.

We first saw the rainbow around the throne of God (Rev. 4:3); now it sits like a crown upon the head of this messenger. The rainbow was God's sign to mankind that He would never again destroy the world with a flood. Even in wrath, God remembers His mercy (Hab. 3:2). Whoever this angel is, he has the authority of God's throne given to him.

God is often identified with clouds. God led Israel by a glorious cloud (Ex. 16:10), and dark clouds covered Sinai when the law was given (19:9). When God appeared to Moses, it was in a cloud of glory (24:15ff; 34:5). "[He] maketh the clouds His chariot" (Ps. 104:3). A cloud received Jesus when He ascended to heaven (Acts 1:9); and, when He returns, it will be with clouds (Rev. 1:7).

The fact that the angel's face is "as the sun" corresponds to the description of Jesus Christ in Revelation 1:16; his feet correspond to the Lord's description in verse 15 of the same chapter. His voice like a lion suggests Revelation 5:5. This being could well be our Lord Jesus Christ, appearing to John as a kingly angel. Jesus often appeared in the Old Testament as "the angel of the Lord" (Ex. 3:2; Jud. 2:4; 6:11-12, 21-22; 2 Sam. 24:16). This was a temporary manifestation for a special purpose, not a permanent incarnation.

Two other characteristics would suggest identifying the angel as Jesus Christ: the book in his hand and the awesome posture that he assumed. The little book contains the rest of the prophetic message that John will deliver. Since our Lord was the only One worthy to take the scroll and break the seals (Rev. 5:5ff), it might well be concluded that He is the only One worthy to give His servant the rest of the message.

The angel's posture is that of a conqueror taking possession of his territory. He is claiming the whole world! (See

Josh. 1:1-3.) Of course, only the victorious Saviour could make such a claim. The Antichrist will soon complete his conquest and force the whole world to submit to his control. But before that happens, the Saviour will claim the world for Himself, the inheritance that His Father promised Him (Ps. 2:6-9). Satan roars like a lion to frighten his prey (1 Peter 5:8), but the Lion of Judah roars to announce victory. (See Ps. 95:3-5; Isa. 40:12-17.)

We are not told why John was forbidden to write what the seven thunders uttered, the only "sealed" thing in an otherwise "unsealed" book (see Dan. 12:9; Rev. 22:10). God's voice is often compared to thunder (John 12:28-29; Ps. 29; Job 26:14; 37:5). It is useless for us to speculate when God chooses to veil His truth (Deut. 29:29).

THE DECLARATION OF THE ANGEL (10:5-7) fills us with awe, not only because of what he declares, but also because of the way he declares it. It is a solemn scene, with his hand lifted to heaven as though he were under oath.

But if this angel is our Lord Jesus Christ, why would He take an oath? In order to affirm the solemnity and certainty of the words spoken. God put Himself "under oath" when He made His covenant with Abraham (Heb. 6:13-20) and when He declared His Son to be high priest (7:20-22). He also took an oath when He promised David that the Christ would come from his family (Acts 2:29-30).

The emphasis in Revelation 10:6 is on God the Creator. Various judgments have already been felt by the heavens, the earth, and the sea; and more judgments are to come. The word that is translated *time* actually means "delay." God has been delaying His judgments so that lost sinners will have time to repent (2 Peter 3:1-9); now, however, He will accelerate His judgments and accomplish His purposes.

Recall that the martyred saints in heaven were concerned about God's seeming delay in avenging their deaths (Rev. 6:10-11). "How long, O Lord, how long?" has been the cry of God's suffering people from age to age. God's seeming delay in fulfilling His promises has given the scoffers opportunity to deny God's Word and question His sincerity (see 2 Peter 3). God's Word is true and His timing, perfect. This means comfort to saints—but judgment to sinners.

In the Bible, a *mystery* is a "sacred secret," a truth hidden to those outside but revealed to God's people by His Word (Matt. 13:10-12). The "mystery of God" has to do with the age-old problem of evil in the world. Why is there both moral and natural evil in the world? Why doesn't God do something about it? Of course, the Christian knows that God did "do something about it" at Calvary when Jesus Christ was made sin and experienced divine wrath for a sinful world. We also know that God is permitting evil to increase until the world is ripe for judgment (2 Thes. 2:7ff; Rev. 14:14-20). Since God has already paid the price for sin, He is free to delay His judgment, and He cannot be accused of injustice or unconcern.

The signal for this mystery's completion is the sounding of the seventh trumpet (11:14-19). The last half of the Tribulation begins when the angels start to pour out the bowls, in which "is filled up [completed] the wrath of God" (15:1).

The directions that the angel gave to John (10:8-11) should remind us of our responsibility to assimilate the Word of God and make it a part of the inner man. It was not enough for John to see the book or even know its contents and purpose. He had to *receive* it into his inner being.

God's Word is compared to food: bread (Matt. 4:4), milk (1 Peter 2:2), meat (1 Cor. 3:1-2), and honey (Ps. 119:103). The Prophets Jeremiah (Jer. 15:16) and Ezekiel (Ezek. 2:9— 3:4) knew what it was to "eat" the Word before they could share it with others. The Word must always "become flesh" (John 1:14) before it can be given to those who need it. Woe unto that preacher or teacher who merely echoes God's Word and does not incarnate it, making it a living part of his very being.

God will not thrust His Word into our mouths and force us to receive it. He hands it to us and we must take it. Nor can He change the effects the Word will have in our lives:

there will be both sorrow and joy, bitterness and sweetness. God's Word contains sweet promises and assurances, but it also contains bitter warnings and prophecies of judgment. The Christian bears witness of both life and death (2 Cor. 2:14-17). The faithful minister will declare all of God's counsel (Acts 20:27). He will not dilute the message of God simply to please his listeners (2 Tim. 4:1-5).

The angel commissioned John to prophesy *again;* his work was not yet completed. He must declare God's prophetic truth concerning (not "before") many peoples, and nations, and tongues, and kings (Rev. 5:9). The word *nations* usually refers to the Gentile nations. John will have much to say about the nations of the world as he presents the rest of this prophecy.

The Testimony of the Two Witnesses (Rev. 11:1-14)

THE MINISTRY OF THE WITNESSES (11:1-6) is described first. The place is Jerusalem and the time is the first half of the Tribulation. Israel is worshiping again at its restored temple, built under the protection of the Antichrist, whose true character has not yet been revealed. To spiritualize verses 1-2 and make the temple refer to the church creates a number of serious problems. For one thing, how could John measure an invisible body of people, even if the church were still on earth? If the temple is the church, then who are the worshipers and what is the altar? And since the church unites Jews and Gentiles in one body (Eph. 2:11ff), why are the Gentiles segregated in this temple? It seems wisest to interpret this temple as an actual building in the holy city of Jerusalem (Neh. 11:1, 18; Dan. 9:24).

John's measurement of the temple is a symbolic action. To measure something means to claim it for yourself. When we sold our house in Chicago, the new owners brought in an architect to measure various areas and recommend possible changes. Had the architect shown up previous to the buyers' commitment, we would have thrown him out. The Lord was saying through John, "I own this city and this temple, and I claim both for Myself!" The Old Testament background is found in Ezekiel 40—41 and Zechariah 2:1-3.

What John did was especially significant because the Gentiles had taken over Jerusalem. Antichrist had broken his agreement with Israel (Dan. 9:27) and now he was about to use the temple for his own diabolical purposes (2 Thes. 2:3-4). All of this will be elaborated in Revelation 13. "Jerusalem shall be trodden down of the Gentiles," said Jesus, "until the times of the Gentiles be fulfilled" (Luke 21:24). The "times of the Gentiles" began in 606 b.c. when Babylon began to devastate Judah and Jerusalem, and it will continue until Jesus Christ returns to deliver the Holy City and redeem Israel (Zech. 14).

Note that the two witnesses minister during the *first* half of the Tribulation (Rev. 11:3; 1,260 days). Jerusalem is then overrun by the Gentiles for forty-two months, the *last* half of the Tribulation.

Their witness is related to Israel and the temple. How tragic that the power of God and the Word of God will be *outside* the temple and not within as in former ages. Like the temple that Jesus left, this new house will be desolate (see Matt. 23:38). These two men are specifically called prophets (Rev. 11:3, 6), and I take this to mean prophetic ministry in the Old Testament sense, calling the nations to repent and return to the true God of Israel.

Not only do these witnesses declare God's words, but they also do God's works and perform miracles of judgment, reminding us of both Moses and Elijah (Ex. 7:14-18; 1 Kings 17:1ff; 2 Kings 1:1-12). Some students cite Malachi 4:5-6 as evidence that one of the witnesses may be Elijah, but Jesus applied that prophecy to John the Baptist (Matt. 17:10-13). John the Baptist, however, denied that he was Elijah returned to earth (John 1:21, 25; see also Luke 1:16-17). This confusion may be explained in part by realizing that throughout Israel's history, God sent special messengers— "Elijahs"—to call His people to repentance; so in this sense, Malachi's prophecy will be fulfilled by the witnesses.

Instead of relating the ministry of the witnesses to Moses and Elijah, the angel who spoke to John connected their ministry with Zerubbabel and Joshua the high priest (Zech. 4). These two men helped to reestablish Israel in Palestine and to rebuild the temple. It was a discouraging task, and the Gentiles made it even more difficult; but God provided the special power they needed to get the work done. This truth is an encouragement to God's servants in all ages, for the work of the Lord is never easy.

THE MARTYRDOM OF THE WITNESSES (11:7-10) comes only when they have finished their testimony. God's obedient servants are immortal until their work is done. "The beast" (Antichrist) is now in power and wants to take over the temple; but he cannot succeed until the two witnesses are out of the way. God will permit him to slay them, for no one will be able to make war against "the beast" and win (Rev. 13:4).

The witnesses will not even be permitted decent burial (see Ps. 79:1-3). But even this indecency will be used by God to bear witness to mankind. No doubt the TV cameras in Jerusalem will transmit the scene to people around the world, and the news analysts will discuss its significance. The earth-dwellers will rejoice at their enemies' removal and will celebrate a "satanic Christmas" by sending gifts to one another. It thus would appear that the power of the two witnesses will not be limited to Jerusalem, but that they will be able to cause things to happen in other parts of the world.

These two prophets will definitely have a relationship with Israel; and the world, for the most part, has not approved of the nation Israel. In the middle of the Tribulation, "the beast" will turn against Israel and begin to persecute the Jews. The two witnesses will not be around to protect the nation and a frightening anti-Semitic movement will ensue.

Jerusalem is called a "great city" (Rev. 11:8); and from a human viewpoint, this is a true statement. But God looks at men and nations from a *spiritual* viewpoint. To Him, Jerusalem will be considered as polluted and worldly as Sodom and as rebellious and proud as Egypt.

THE RESURRECTION OF THE WITNESSES (11:11-14). Miraculously, the two witnesses are not only raised from the dead, but caught up into heaven! God rescues them from their enemies and gives a solemn witness to the watching world. The world's great joy suddenly becomes great fear. (Note the word *great* in chapter 11, repeated eight times.)

Are we to interpret the three and a half days literally? Or does the phrase simply mean "after a short time"? It seems too specific to mean that. Does it symbolize a longer period, say three and a half years? It is not likely that two dead bodies would be kept lying in a city street for more than three years. Perhaps this is a picture of a rapture of all the saints in the midst of the Tribulation, and the three and a half years covers the first half of the period. If so, then what is symbolized by the *death* of the two witnesses? This interpretation solves one problem only to create another.

These days appear to be literal days, just as the forty-two months in Revelation 11:2 are literal months. The Bible does not explain why this length of time was chosen and it is useless for us to speculate.

Our Lord's *friends* watched Him ascend to heaven (Acts 1:9-12), but the witnesses' *enemies* will see them resurrected and will be shaken with fear. Their fear will increase when a great earthquake occurs, killing 7,000 men and destroying a tenth part of Jerusalem. A great earthquake occurred when the sixth seal was opened (Rev. 6:12), and there will be a greater one when the seventh vial is poured out (16:18-20).

The Testimony of the Elders (Rev. 11:15-19)
We have been waiting since Revelation 8:13 for this third "woe" to arrive and now it is here. When the seventh angel blew the trumpet, three dramatic events occurred.

AN ANNOUNCEMENT OF VICTORY (11:15). These "great voices" were probably the choirs of heaven. The great announcement is that the kingdom (John uses the singular because "the beast" now has the world under his control) of this world belongs to Jesus Christ. Of course, Christ does not *claim* His royal rights until He returns; but the victory has already been won. Satan offered Him the world's kingdoms, but He refused the offer (Matt. 4:8-9). Instead, He died on the cross, arose, and returned victoriously to heaven; and there the Father gave Him His inheritance (Ps. 2:4-9).

However, we must not incorrectly assume that our Lord is not reigning *today*, because He is. According to Hebrews 7:1-2, Jesus Christ is "King of righteousness" and "King of peace." He is enthroned with the Father (Rev. 3:21), and He will reign until He defeats all His foes (1 Cor. 15:25). Today, He rules over a spiritual kingdom; but in that future day, He will reign over the nations of the world and rule with a rod of iron.

No matter how difficult the circumstances might be, or how defeated God's people may think they are, Jesus Christ is still King of kings and Lord of lords, and He is in control. One day, we shall triumph!

AN ACCLAMATION OF PRAISE (11:16-18). The elders left their own thrones and prostrated themselves in worship before God's throne. They gave thanks for three special blessings: that Christ reigns supremely (v. 17), that He judges righteously (v. 18), and that He rewards graciously (v. 18).

In Revelation 4:10-11, the elders praised the Creator; and in 5:9-14, they worshiped the Redeemer. Here the emphasis is on the Conqueror and the King. Keep in mind that the church on earth looked as though it were defeated, for Rome was the conqueror and king. John was reminding the saints that *they* were "a kingdom of priests" reigning with the Saviour (1:5-6). It may seem at times that the throne of heaven is empty, but it is not. Jesus Christ has both power and authority—in fact, *all* authority (Matt. 28:18, where the word *power* means "authority"). "Thou . . . hast begun to reign" is a good translation.

Christ not only reigns supremely, but He judges righteously (Rev. 11:18). The Lamb is also the Lion! In verse 18, we have a "table of contents" for the remainder of the Book of Revelation. These events did not take place the instant the angel blew his trumpet; he simply signaled the beginning of the process, and now these events would take place as planned.

"The nations were angry." What do the nations have to be angry about? Certainly the Lord has been good and gracious to them. He has provided their needs (Acts 14:15-17; 17:24-31), assigned their territories, and graciously postponed His judgment to give men opportunity to be saved. Even more, He sent His Son to be the Saviour of the world. Today, God offers forgiveness to the nations! What more could He do for them?

Then, why are the nations angry? *Because they want to have their own way.* "Why do the heathen [the nations] rage, and the people imagine a vain thing? The kings of the earth set themselves, and the rulers take counsel together, against the Lord, and against His anointed [Christ], saying, 'Let us break Their bands asunder, and cast away Their cords from us' " (Ps. 2:1-3). They want to worship and serve the creature instead of the Creator (Rom. 1:25). Like adolescent children, the nations want to cast off all restraint; *and God will permit them to do so.* The result will be another "Babylon" (Rev. 17—18), man's last attempt to build his Utopia, a "heaven on earth."

Note the change in attitude shown by the nations of the world. In Revelation 11:2, the nations ruthlessly take over Jerusalem. In 11:9, they rejoice at the death of the two witnesses. But now, they are angry; their arrogance and joy did not last very long. This belligerent attitude finally will cause the nations to unite to fight God at the great battle of Armageddon.

"And Thy wrath is come." The word translated *angry* in verse 18 is the verb form of the word translated *wrath.* But man's wrath can never equal the wrath of the Lamb (6:16-17). Even Satan's wrath, as cruel as it is, is no match for God's wrath (12:17). There was intense suffering in the first half of the Tribulation, but only the last half will reveal the wrath of God (11:18; 14:10; 16:19; 19:15). There are two Greek words for anger: *thumos*, which means "rage, passionate anger," and *orgē*, used here, which means "indignation, a settled attitude of wrath." God's anger is not an outburst of temper; it is holy indignation against sin. Both of these Greek words are used in Revelation to describe God's anger: *orgē* is used only four times; *thumos*, seven (14:10, 19; 15:1, 7; 16:1, 19; 19:15). God's anger is not dispassionate, for He hates sin and loves righteousness and justice; but neither is it tempermental and unpredictable.

"And the time of the dead, that they should be judged" takes us to the very end of God's prophetic program. In one sense, every day is a "day of the Lord" because God is always judging righteously. God is long-suffering toward lost sinners and often postpones judgment, but there will be a final judgment of sinners and none will escape. This judgment is described in Revelation 20:11-15.

There will also be a judgment of God's children, known as "the Judgment Seat of Christ" (Rom. 14:10-13; 1 Cor. 3:9-15; 2 Cor. 5:9-11). God will reward His faithful servants (Matt. 25:21) and the sufferings they experienced on earth will be forgotten in the glory of His presence. Though God's children will not be judged for their sins (that judgment took place on the cross), they will be judged for their works and rewarded generously by the Master.

The Judgment Seat of Christ will take place in heaven after Christ has called His people home. When He returns to earth to establish His kingdom, the saints will be ready to reign with Him, with every blemish of the church removed (Eph. 5:25-27; Rev. 19:7-8). Today, we groan as we serve God, because we know only too well our handicaps and blemishes; but one day, we shall serve Him *perfectly!*

"Them that destroy the earth" refers to the rebellious earth-dwellers who will not submit to God. How ironic that these people live for the earth and its pleasures, yet at the same time are *destroying* the very earth that they worship!

When man forgets that God is the Creator and he is the creature, he begins to exploit his God-given resources, and this brings destruction. Man is a steward of creation, not the owner.

As mentioned before, verse 18 is a summary statement of events yet to come. It is heaven's song of praise for the Lord's faithfulness to accomplish His purposes in the world. Again, it appears strange to us that heavenly beings can sing about judgment. Perhaps if we had more of the throne's perspective, we would be able to join their praises.

AN ASSURANCE OF GOD'S FAITHFULNESS (11:19). This chapter opened with a temple on earth, but now we see the temple in heaven. The focus of attention is on the ark of God, the symbol of God's presence with His people.

In the Old Testament tabernacle and temple, the ark stood behind the veil, in the holy of holies. God's glory rested on the ark, and God's Law was within the ark, beautifully illustrating that the two must never be separated. He is a holy God and must deal righteously with sin. But He is also a faithful God who keeps His promises to His people. It was the ark of God that led Israel through the Jordan and into their inheritance (Josh. 3:11-17). This vision of the ark would greatly encourage God's suffering people to whom John sent this book. "God will fulfill His promises!" John was saying to them. "He will reveal His glory! Trust Him!"

Once again, John saw and heard the portents of a storm (see Rev. 4:5; 8:5). Greater judgment is about to fall on the rebellious people of earth! But God's people need not fear the storms for He is in control. The ark reminds them of His presence and the faithfulness of His promises. And on that ark was the mercy seat on which the blood was sprinkled each Day of Atonement (Lev. 16:15-17). Even in wrath, God remembers His mercy (Hab. 3:2).

The stage is now set for the dramatic appearance of "the beast," Satan's masterpiece, the false Christ who will control the world.

8

The Terrible Trio

Revelation 12—13

Revelation 12—13 introduces us to the three key characters in the drama of the last half of the Tribulation: Satan the dragon, the false Christ, and the false prophet. These three are, in a sense, an evil trinity, opposing the true God and His people on earth. While these events will be of special significance to God's people at that time, the message of these two chapters can encourage suffering saints during any age.

Satan is the great enemy of the church, and he fights against God and His people by accusing the saints in heaven and attacking them on earth. However, Christ has overcome the old serpent, and He gives victory to His people.

The adversary always works through human means, in this case, "the beast" (false Christ or Antichrist) and the false prophet. Satan is an imitator, a counterfeiter; and he seeks to control men by means of deception. "The beast" is the future world dictator who promises to solve the pressing problems of the nations; the false prophet is his "propaganda minister." For a time, it appears that the satanic trio is succeeding; but then their world empire begins to collapse, the nations assemble for one final battle, Jesus Christ appears, and the battle is over.

Has this not been the pattern for the church's conflict

with evil over the centuries? Whether the ruler has been a Caesar, a Hitler, a Stalin, or an agnostic humanist, Satan has energized and motivated him. The ruler has promised the people all that they want and need, only to lead them into slavery. He has usually had an associate to promote his program to the people and to entice them, if not force them, to obey. Often their submission amounted almost to worship.

God has permitted His people to suffer under the despotism of these rulers, but He has also enabled His people to experience great victories, even in martyrdom. They have been true overcomers! Then He has brought deliverance, only to have the cycle repeat itself, with each succeeding dictatorship worse than the previous one. The climax will come with the appearance of the Antichrist in his time (2 Thes. 2).

The Dragon (Rev. 12)

John's vision opens with *two wonders in heaven* (12:1-6). The first is a woman giving birth to a son. Since this child is identified as Jesus Christ (compare v. 5 with Rev. 19:15 and Ps. 2:9), this symbolic woman can be none other than the nation Israel. It was through Israel that Jesus Christ came into the world (Rom. 1:3; 9:4-5). By further comparing the description in Revelation 12:1 with Genesis 37:9-10, the identification seems certain.

In the Old Testament, Israel is often compared to a woman, and even a woman in travail (Isa. 54:5; 66:7; Jer. 3:6-10; Micah 4:10; 5:2-3). The apostate world system is compared to a harlot (Rev. 17:1ff), and the church to a pure bride (19:7ff).

The son is born and is then caught up to the throne of God (12:5). We have symbolized here the birth of Christ and His victorious ascension, but nothing is said about either His life or His death. The colon in the middle of the verse represents thirty-three years of history!

The woman with child is the first wonder; the great red dragon is the second. Verse 9 makes it clear that this is

Satan. The color red is associated with death (6:4) and Satan is a murderer (John 8:44). The heads, horns, and crowns will appear again in Revelation 13:1 and 17:3. The heads represent mountains (17:9), and the horns represent kings (17:12). We shall study the meaning of these symbols in more detail later.

The dragon was cast out of heaven (12:9), and he took with him a third of the angels (vv. 7, 9). They are spoken of as "stars" in verse 4 (see also Dan. 8:10). This is evidently a reference to the fall of Satan (Isa. 14:12-15), when he and his hosts revolted against God. However, the casting out described in Revelation 12:7-10 is yet future.

Just as soon as the child was born, Satan tried to destroy Him. This conflict between Satan and "the woman" began soon after man fell (Gen. 3:15). Throughout Old Testament history, Satan tried to prevent the birth of the Redeemer. There was always a "dragon" standing by, waiting to destroy Israel or the ancestors of the Messiah. Pharaoh is called a "dragon" (Ezek. 29:3), and so is Nebuchadnezzar (Jer. 51:34). At one critical point, the royal line was limited to one little boy! (2 Kings 11:1-3) When Jesus Christ was born, Satan used King Herod to try to destroy Him (Matt. 2). Satan thought that he had succeeded when he used Judas to betray the Lord and hand Him over to be crucified. But the Cross was actually Satan's defeat! "And they overcame him [Satan] by the blood of the Lamb" (Rev. 12:11).

Even today Satan has access to heaven, where he accuses God's people; but he cannot dethrone the exalted Saviour. His strategy is to persecute God's people and devour them if possible (1 Peter 5:8). He has a special hatred for the Jewish people and has been the power behind anti-Semitism from the days of Pharaoh and Haman (see the Book of Esther) to Hitler and Stalin. Finally, in the middle of the Tribulation, there will come a wave of anti-Semitism such as the world has never seen (Rev. 12:6). But God will protect His people during those three and a half years (1,260 days; see 11:2; 13:5).

Apart from the 144,000 (who are sealed and protected), a believing remnant of Jews will survive this very troublesome time. We are not told where God will protect them or who it is that will care for them. Matthew 24:15-21 will take on special meaning for those believing Jews who live in the end days. Note especially the parenthesis in verse 15.

You and I are involved in a similar conflict today (see Eph. 6:10ff). Satan is out to destroy the church, and our victory can come only through Jesus Christ.

The next scene in this cosmic drama is *a war in heaven* (Rev. 12:7-12). Scripture makes it clear that Satan has access to heaven even today (Job 1—2). Once he was the highest of God's angels, but he rebelled against God and was cast down (Isa. 14:12-15). Interestingly, as God's church faithfully serves Christ and wins the lost, Satan is also cast down and defeated (Luke 10:1-2, 17-20; Matt. 16:18; note also 12:29).

Of course, when Jesus Christ died on the cross, it meant Satan's ultimate defeat (John 12:31-33). Satan will one day be cast out of heaven (Rev. 12:7-10), and then finally cast into hell (20:10).

What is this celestial conflict all about? The fact that Michael led God's angels to victory is significant, because Michael is identified with the nation Israel (Dan. 10:10-21; 12:1; note also Jude 9). The name *Michael* means "who is like God?" and this certainly parallels Satan's egocentric attack on Jehovah—"I will be like the Most High" (Isa. 14:14). Apparently, the devil's hatred of Israel will spur him to make one final assault against the throne of God, but he will be defeated by Michael and a heavenly host.

But perhaps there is another factor involved in this war. After the church is taken to heaven, believers will stand before the Judgment Seat of Christ and have their works examined. On the basis of this judgment, rewards will be given (Rom. 14:10-12; 1 Cor. 3:10-15; 2 Cor. 5:10-11). It seems likely that Satan will be present at this event and will accuse the saints, pointing out all the "spots and wrinkles" in the church (Eph. 5:24-27).

The name *devil* means "accuser," and *Satan* means "adversary." Satan stands at the throne of God and fights the saints by accusing them (see Job 1—2; Zech. 3). But Jesus Christ, the "heavenly advocate" (1 John 2:1-2), represents the church before God's holy throne. Because Jesus Christ died for us, we can overcome Satan's accusations "by the blood of the Lamb." Our salvation is secure, not because of our own works, but because of His finished work at Calvary.

How furious Satan will be when the church comes forth in glory "without spot or wrinkle, or any such thing." When the accuser sees that his tactics have failed, he will become angry and threaten the very peace of heaven.

How does this future war apply to the church today? The same serpent who accuses the saints in heaven also deceives the nations on earth (Rev. 12:9); and one of his strategies is to lie about the church. He deceives the nations into thinking that the people of God are dangerous, deluded, even destructive. It is through Satan's deception that the leaders of the nations band together against Christ and His people (Ps. 2; Acts 4:23-30). God's people *in every age* must expect the world's opposition, but the church can always defeat the enemy by being faithful to Jesus Christ.

Christ's shed blood gives us our perfect standing before God (1 John 1:5—2:2). But our witness to God's Word and our willingness to lay down our lives for Christ defeats Satan as well. Satan is not equal to God; he is not omnipotent, omnipresent, or omniscient. His power is limited and his tactics must fail when God's people trust the power of the blood and of the Word. Nothing Satan does can rob us of "salvation, and strength, and the kingdom of our God, and the power of His Christ" (Rev. 12:10), if we are yielded to Him. God's great purposes will be fulfilled!

Believers in any age or situation can rejoice in this victory, no matter how difficult their experiences may be. Our warfare is not against flesh and blood, but against the spiritual forces of the wicked one; and these have been defeated by our Saviour (Eph. 6:10ff; note also 1:15-23).

Heaven will rejoice when Satan is cast out, but the earth-dwellers will not; for the last half of the Tribulation will mean intense suffering for the world. The "woe" in Rev. 12:12 reminds us of the "three woes" referred to in 8:13. The first "woe" is described in 9:1-12, and the second in 9:13-21. The third "woe" is referred to in 11:14ff, but this passage only summarizes the events that will climax God's plan for the earth. It may be that part of this third "woe" is casting out Satan and permitting his terrible wrath on earth.

This, then, is the third scene in the drama: *Satan's wrath on earth* (12:13-16). Knowing that his time is short, and having no more access to heaven, the adversary must vent all of his anger earthward. He begins with Israel (the woman), and creates a wave of anti-Semitism. Satan has always hated the Jews because they are God's chosen people and the vehicle through which salvation came into the world. Satan would like to destroy the nation, particularly as the time draws near for the Messiah to return to earth to establish the promised kingdom. A Jewish remnant must be ready to receive Him and form the nucleus for the kingdom (Rev. 1:7; Zech. 12:9—14:21).

God will prepare a special place where the Jewish remnant will be protected and cared for. It is interesting that the remnant's escape from Satan is described in terms of a flying eagle, for this is a repeated image in the Old Testament with reference to Israel. God delivered Israel from Egypt "on eagles' wings" (Ex. 19:4), and cared for the people in the wilderness as an eagle would her young (Deut. 32:11-12). Their return from Babylonian captivity was like "mounting up with wings as eagles" (Isa. 40:31).

Note that the remnant will be sheltered for the last half of the Tribulation. We do not know where this sheltered place will be, nor do we need to know. But the lesson for all of us is clear: God cares for those whom He wants to use to accomplish His purposes on earth. True, some people will give their lives (Rev. 12:11), but others will be spared. (See Acts

12 for an example of this principle.)

The phrase "water as a flood" is not explained, but there is a parallel in Psalm 124. (Also note the phrase "escaped as a bird" in verse 7 of this same Psalm.) This "flood" is probably an outpouring of hatred and anti-Semitic propaganda. Or it may symbolize armies that invade Israel and seek to defeat the remnant. If that is the meaning, then the earth opening up could well be an earthquake that God sends to destroy the invaders. When Satan discovers that the people he seeks to kill are protected, then he turns on those who were not carried to the hidden place of safety. He will declare war, and God will permit him to have victory for a time (Rev. 13:7); but ultimately, the old serpent will be defeated.

The Beast from the Sea (Rev. 13:1-10)

Some texts read, "And he [Satan] stood upon the sand of the sea." The sea symbolizes the Gentile nations (17:15). From one of them, Satan will bring forth his "Super Leader," the man we call "Antichrist." Up to this point, Antichrist has headed a ten-nation European league; but now he is about to embark on a new career as Satan's world dictator.

You will remember that Antichrist began his career as a peacemaker (6:2) and even "settled" the Arab-Israeli problem by making a covenant with the Jews to protect them for seven years (Dan. 9:27). This protection would permit the nation to rebuild the temple and reinstitute religious rituals (Rev. 11:1; Dan. 9:27). But in the middle of the seven-year period (the time we are studying now in Revelation 10—14) he will break that covenant, stop the ceremonies, and set up himself as god in the temple (Dan. 9:27; 2 Thes. 2:1-12).

The symbolic description of "the beast" enables us to learn something about his origin and character. God does not see him as a man, made in the divine image, but as a wild animal, under the control of Satan. He is a man (Rev. 13:18); but he is energized from hell, for he comes out of the pit (11:7; 17:8). Just as Jesus Christ is God in the flesh, so "the beast" will be Satan in a human body. (See John 13:2, 27.)

The seven heads represent seven mountains (Rev. 17:9); and since Rome was built on seven hills, this must be a veiled reference to that powerful city (see 17:18). It would be a most meaningful allusion in John's day!

The ten horns represent ten kingdoms (Dan. 7:24; Rev. 17:12). It appears that "the beast" will head a "United States of Europe," a revived Roman Empire, before taking over as world dictator. All nations will no doubt admire and thank him for the "peace" he has achieved, little realizing the sorrow and destruction he will bring to the world.

The three animals named in Revelation 13:2 remind us of the four beasts Daniel saw in his dream (Dan. 7): a lion (Babylon), a bear (Media-Persia), a leopard (Greece), and a "terrible beast" (the Antichrist). John saw these animals, or kingdoms, in reverse order since he was looking *back*, while Daniel was looking *ahead*. The final world empire will be rooted in all the previous empires and unite in one their evil and power. Added to the ferocity of these beasts will be Satan's own power, throne, and authority!

Once Satan presents his great "masterpiece," the counterfeit Christ, to the world, what will happen next?

First, there will be *wonder* (Rev. 13:3). Certainly a terrified world will wonder at Antichrist's power and his sudden rise to international fame and authority. But mankind will also wonder at the healing of his "wound." What is this "wound"? John does not explain it, but perhaps what he later wrote (17:9-13) can help interpret the symbolism. This "wound" must be important, because John mentioned it three times (vv. 3, 12, 14), including the fact that it was sword-inflicted.

The seven heads represent seven mountains, but also seven kings or kingdoms (17:10). Antichrist or "the beast" is one of these seven kings (17:11), but he is also the eighth. Apparently, he reigns twice; but how can this be? The suggestion has been made that "the beast" will be a European leader who will form a ten-nation federation (17:12), but be slain in the process. Revelation 11:7 and 17:8 state that "the beast" will ascend out of the abyss. Is it possible that Satan will (with God's permission) resurrect a man from the dead? If Satan has power to give life to a dead idol (13:15), could he not also give life to a dead body?

If "the beast" ruled as one of the seven kings, was slain, and then raised up again, he could rule as the eighth king. If, on the other hand, the image is seen representing *kingdoms* rather than individuals, we would have the reemergence of a "dead kingdom" on the world scene. However, it would be difficult to understand how a kingdom could be slain by a sword. It is best, I think, to apply this prophecy to individual persons.

Not only will there be wonder, but there will also be *worship* (13:4). Worship is the one thing Satan has always wanted (Matt. 4:8-10), and he will receive it through "the beast." The second "beast," described in the last half of this chapter, will organize and promote the worship of Antichrist, making it the official religion of the world!

There will also be *words* (13:5-6). Almost all dictators have risen to power by controlling people with their words. Some of us can recall when Adolf Hitler was rising to power, and how he mesmerized huge crowds with his speeches. Satan will make "the beast" a great orator, whose addresses will blaspheme God, His name, His tabernacle (heaven), and the saints in heaven. Since Satan will have recently been cast out of heaven, this blasphemy is to be expected.

Satan can do nothing without God's permission (see Job 1—2; Luke 22:31-32), so "the beast's" authority is *delegated*, not inherent. It will last for three and a half years, the last half of the Tribulation.

In his night vision, Daniel saw "the beast" as the fourth and final empire (Dan. 7:19-28). There, as in John's vision, is the same image of the ten horns with the added revelation that "the beast" must defeat three of the kings to gain control. Daniel also heard "the beast's" blasphemous words (7:25).

Finally, there will be *war* (Rev. 13:7-10). God will permit Antichrist to war against His people ("wear out the saints," Dan. 7:25) and even to defeat some of them. John prophesied that some of the saints will be captured and some will be martyred. But because of their faith, they will have patience, or endurance (see Heb. 6:12; Rev. 1:9), and will not deny the Lord in spite of persecution and death.

The world's population will be divided: those who are saved, with their names in God's book, will not submit to "the beast"; those who are lost—the earth-dwellers—will worship "the beast" and do his bidding. Note that Revelation 13:9 applies this truth to "any man," no matter in which age he may live. Certainly in John's day, this was meaningful; for every Roman citizen had to acknowledge, "Caesar is Lord." Likewise in every age of the church, true believers have had to take their stand for Christ, come what may.

Keep in mind that "the beast" is a counterfeit Christ. The world would not receive Christ, but it will receive Antichrist (John 5:43). The world would not believe the truth, but they will believe the lie (2 Thes. 2:8-12). Jesus spoke (and still speaks) gracious words of salvation, and men turn a deaf ear; but they will listen to the blasphemous words of "the beast." The world will not worship *the* Christ, but they will bow down to Antichrist.

In Revelation 17, we will learn that "the beast" rises to power by means of "the harlot," a symbol of the apostate world church. This is not any one denomination or faith, but a world religious system that has rejected God's Son and God's truth. However, when "the beast" rises to universal power, he will no longer need "the harlot" and shall subsequently destroy her and establish his own satanic religion.

The Beast from the Earth (Rev. 13:11-18)

In Rev. 16:13, 19:20, and 20:10, the beast from the earth is called "the false prophet." The dragon or Satan is the counterfeit Father ("I will be like the Most High"), "the beast" is the counterfeit Christ, and the false prophet is the counterfeit Holy Spirit. This completes the satanic trinity.

One of the ministries of the Holy Spirit is to glorify Christ and lead people to trust and worship Him (John 16:7-15). The false prophet will point to Antichrist and his image and compel people to worship Satan through "the beast."

The image of the horns (Rev. 13:11) suggests that the false prophet has authority, but the absence of a crown indicates that his authority is not political. Our Lord warned that there would be false prophets (Matt. 24:11, 24), and this one will be the greatest. He will have the "character" of a lamb but the voice of the dragon. What a deceiver he will be—and all the world will listen to him!

When our Lord ministered on earth, Jewish leaders often asked Him to perform some sign to prove that He was indeed their Messiah; and Jesus refused. But the false prophet will perform deceptive signs that will lead the world into devil-worship (see 2 Thes. 2:9). His greatest sign will be "the abomination of desolation" mentioned by Daniel (Dan. 9:27; 11:36), Jesus (Matt. 24:15), and Paul (2 Thes. 2:4).

What is "the abomination of desolation"? It is the image of "the beast," set up in the temple in Jerusalem. An idol is bad enough; but setting it up in the temple is the height of all blasphemy. Since Satan could not command worship in heaven, he will go to the next best place—the Jewish temple in the Holy City. (See Dan. 8:9-14.)

The false prophet, energized by Satan, will perform his "lying wonders" and even duplicate some of the signs performed by the two witnesses (Rev. 13:13; see also 11:5). Up to this time, the two witnesses have been ministering at the temple in Jerusalem, but "the beast" will slay them and take over the temple. When God raises the two witnesses from the dead and takes them to heaven, the false prophet will answer that challenge by giving life to the image of "the beast." Not only will the image move, but it will speak!

Not content to control people through religious deceit, the false prophet will institute strong economic measures as well. Everybody (except believers; 20:4) will receive a special mark in order to buy or sell; but the only way to get that mark is to submit to "the beast" and worship him. Surely this is a strong allusion to the Caesar worship in the Roman Empire, but this same policy has been used by political leaders throughout history.

This special mark is the name or number of "the beast"— the mystical 666. In the ancient world, the letters of the alphabet were used for numbers, both in Greek and Hebrew; and Bible students have been attempting for years to unravel the mystery of this name and number. If you work at it hard enough, almost *any* name will fit!

Since man was created on the sixth day, six is the number of man. Creation was made for man and likewise has the number six stamped on it: twenty-four hours to a day (4 x 6), twelve months to a year (2 x 6). Seven is the number of perfection and fullness, but six is the "human number," just short of perfection.

Despite all man's imaginative calculations, we must confess that no one knows the meaning of this number and name. No doubt believers on earth at that time will understand it clearly. The "satanic trinity" cannot claim the number seven; it must settle for 666.

This much is sure: in recent years, we have seen a worldwide increase in the use of numbers for identification. In the United States, a person's Social Security number is indispensable. In fact, numbers are more important to computers than names! Perhaps this is an advance warning of what will happen on earth when "the beast" is in control.

We have reached the middle of the Tribulation in our study, but we are not yet ready for the return of the Lord. Before John revealed how the great drama will climax, he paused to overview great events to come; and that will be our next topic.

An antichristian system pervades our world, and true believers must not be a part of it (1 John 2:15-17). We must shun false worship (1 Cor. 10:14-22), that we may be found faithful to the Lord in these last days! (2 Tim. 3)

9

Voices of Victory

Revelation 14—16

One of the themes that links Revelation 14—16 together is expressed by the word *voice*, which is used eleven times. In the events recorded, God speaks to His people or to the lost world, or His creatures speak out in praise of the Lord or in warning to the world. As the world moves into the last half of the Tribulation, heaven is not silent.

The Voice of the 144,000 (Rev. 14:1-5)

This special group of Jewish men was sealed by God before the seventh seal was opened (Rev. 7), and now they are seen on Mount Zion with the Lord Jesus Christ. Contrast this picture to the one described in Revelation 13: the followers of "the beast" whose mark is on their foreheads (v. 16). God always has His faithful people, no matter how wicked the world may become.

The 144,000 are *standing* with Christ on Mount Zion, but which Mount Zion: the heavenly one (Heb. 12:22-24) or the earthly one? I personally believe that this is the heavenly Mount Zion, and that the scene anticipates Christ's coronation and the establishment of His kingdom when He returns to earth (Zech. 14:4ff). Christ today is enthroned in the heavenly Zion (Ps. 2:6), and we are enthroned with Him

(Eph. 2:6). The scene in Revelation 14 is the assurance to God's people that He cares for His own and finally will take them to glory.

Not only are the 144,000 standing, but they are also *singing* (Rev. 14:2-3). Because of the special experiences they had during the Tribulation, they have a new song to sing that others cannot share. (See Pss. 33:3; 40:3; 96:1; 98:1; 144:9; 149:1.) They are accompanied by heavenly harps and other heavenly voices. It is encouraging to know that one day our sorrows will be transformed into songs!

John also pointed out their *separation* (Rev. 14:4-5). The 144,000 did not belong *to* the earth because they had been redeemed *out of* the earth. They were not earth-dwellers, but citizens of heaven. Believers today do not belong to this very special group, but, like them, we have been redeemed and are not part of this world system. (See John 17:14-19; Phil. 3:17-21.)

The phrase "defiled with women" does not imply that sex within marriage is evil, because it is not (Heb. 13:4). It merely indicates that these 144,000 Jewish men were unmarried. In the Bible, fornication and adultery are pictures of idolatry (Ex. 34:15; James 4:4). While most of the world bowed down to the image of "the beast," the 144,000 were faithful to the true God. While others lied to get what they needed, the 144,000 were without guile and blemish.

The term *firstfruits* means "the very finest." But it also carries the idea of an expected harvest. On the Feast of Firstfruits, the priest waved the sheaf before the Lord as a sign that the entire harvest belonged to Him (Lev. 23:9-14). The 144,000 may be the firstfruits of the harvest yet to come; they may be the nucleus of the coming kingdom. However, it would seem difficult for a *heavenly* company such as this to establish an earthly kingdom.

The Voices of the Angels (Rev. 14:6-20)
At least six different angels are involved in this scene, each with a particular message to proclaim.

"JUDGMENT IS COME!" (14:6-7) During the present age, the angels are not privileged to preach the Gospel. That responsibility has been given to God's people. While the nations will fear "the beast" and give honor to him, this heavenly messenger will summon them to fear and honor God alone. It is a reminder that God is the Creator and He alone deserves worship. This is not the Gospel message as we know it (1 Cor. 15:1-4); rather, it is a return to the message of Romans 1:18ff, what theologians call "natural theology."

All creation bears witness to God's existence as well as to His power and wisdom. Nonetheless, "the beast" will convince men that he is in charge of the world, and that their destinies are in his hands. The message of the angel calls men back to basics: God is Creator—worship and serve Him. The fear of the Lord, not the fear of "the beast," is the source of wisdom (Prov. 9:10).

"BABYLON IS FALLEN!" (14:8) This proclamation anticipates the events of Revelation 18 (see also 16:18-19). We will consider it in detail then. "Babylon" is God's name for the world system of "the beast," the entire economic and political organization by which he rules. "The harlot" (Rev. 17) is the religious system that "the beast" uses to help build his organization. When Antichrist establishes his own religion (13:11-15), he will destroy the "harlot"; but it is God who will destroy Babylon.

"ESCAPE GOD'S WRATH!" (14:9-13) The third message is directed especially to those who are deciding about following "the beast." It is a warning that "the easy way" is really the hard way, that to "go along with the world" means to go away from God. The Greek text reads, "If any man continues to worship the beast," suggesting that there is still opportunity for repentance and salvation.

"Drinking the cup" is sometimes used as an image of judgment (Jer. 25:15ff; 51:7ff; note also Rev. 14:8). God's final judgments on mankind will be "vials of wrath" poured out from heaven (Rev. 16). God will not mix mercy with this judgment (Ps. 75:8; Hab. 3:2), but will pour out His undiluted indignation on a rebellious world.

Images like "fire and brimstone" (Rev. 14:10) and "smoke" (14:11) upset some people. They ask, "How can a God of love actually permit His creatures to suffer eternal torment?" But we must keep in mind that God's love is a *holy* love, not one based on sentimentality, and therefore He *must* justly deal with sin. We may not like the word *torment*, but it is here just the same (v. 10; see also 9:5; 11:10; 20:10).

We must also keep in mind that God has repeatedly warned sinners and given them opportunity to repent. The first angel in this series invited sinners to turn to God, and the second one warned that the whole "Babylonian" system would be destroyed. If people persist in their sins even after God sends judgments and warnings, then they have only themselves to blame.

John intended for his readers to see the contrast between verses 11 and 13: no rest for the wicked, but eternal rest for the saints (see 2 Thes. 1:3-12). Better to reign with Christ forever than with Antichrist for a few short years! Better to endure persecution patiently now than to escape it and suffer throughout eternity!

"THE HARVEST IS RIPE!" (14:14-20) The person pictured here on the white cloud is undoubtedly our Lord Jesus Christ (see Dan. 7:13-14; Rev. 1:13). We have had the image of the cup, and now we have the image of the harvest, both of the grain (vv. 14-16) and of the grape (vv. 17-20). Again, this anticipates the final judgment of the world.

While winning lost souls to Christ is sometimes pictured as a harvest (John 4:34-38), this image is also used of God's judgment (Luke 3:8-17; Matt. 13:24-30, 36-43). God permits the seeds of iniquity to grow until they are ripe, and then He judges (Gen. 15:16).

The grape harvest is often a picture of judgment (see Joel 3:13ff, which anticipates the Day of the Lord). In actuality, Scripture portrays three different "vines." Israel was God's vine, planted in the land to bear fruit for God's glory; but the nation failed God and had to be cut down (Ps. 80:8-16; Isa.

5:1-7; see also Matt. 21:33-46). Today, Christ is the Vine and believers are branches in Him (John 15). But the world system is also a vine, "the vine of the earth" in contrast to Christ, the heavenly Vine; and it is ripening for judgment. The wicked system—Babylon—that intoxicates people and controls them, will one day be cut down and destroyed in "the winepress of the wrath of God."

Some see in this image an anticipation of the "battle of Armageddon," when the armies of the world will gather against Jerusalem (Zech. 14:1-4; Rev. 16:16). Certainly, John is using hyperbole when he describes a river of blood four feet deep and 200 miles long. (See also Isa. 63:1-6.) Today, God is speaking to the world in grace, and men will not listen. One day hence, He must speak in wrath. The bitter cup will be drunk, the harvest of sin reaped, and the vine of the earth cut down and cast into the winepress.

The Voice of the Victors (Rev. 15:1-4)

At this point, John saw the seven angels holding the seven vials of God's wrath, poised for action. The wicked world is about to "drink of the wine of the wrath of God" (14:10); but before the angels pour out their judgments, there is an "interlude" of blessing. Before sending the "third woe" (11:14), God once again reassures His faithful people.

John saw the believers from the Tribulation who had overcome "the beast" and his system. These are the people who "loved not their lives unto the death" (12:11). Since they did not cooperate with the satanic system and receive the mark of "the beast," they were unable to buy or sell (13:17). They were totally dependent on the Lord for their daily bread. Some of them were put into prison and some were slain (13:10); but all of them practiced faith and patience.

This entire scene is reminiscent of Israel following the Exodus. The nation had been delivered from Egypt by the blood of the lamb, and the Egyptian army had been destroyed at the Red Sea. In thankfulness to God, the Israelites stood by the sea and sang "the song of Moses."

The Tribulation saints whom John saw and heard were standing by the "sea of glass" in heaven (4:6), just as the Israelites stood by the Red Sea. They were singing "the song of Moses" and also "the song of the Lamb." "The song of Moses" is recorded in Exodus 15, and its refrain is: "The Lord is my strength and song, and He is become my salvation" (v. 2). The 144,000 sang a song that nobody else could sing; but this is a song *all* saints can sing.

When Israel returned from Babylonian captivity and reestablished their government and restored temple worship, they used this same refrain at the dedication services (Ps. 118; see especially v. 14).

In the future, when God shall call His people back to their land, Isaiah prophesied that they will sing this song again! (Isa. 11:15—12:6) "The song of Moses" is indeed an important song in the hymnal of the Jewish nation.

This scene would give great assurance and endurance to suffering saints in any age of the church. It is possible to be victorious over the world system! One does not have to yield to the "mark of the beast." Through the blood of the Lamb, we have deliverance. Our Lord's work on the cross is a "spiritual exodus" accomplished by His blood. (Note Luke 9:31, where the word *decease* is *exodus* in the Greek.)

In their song, the Tribulation saints praise God's works as well as His ways. The earth-dwellers certainly would not praise God for His works, and they would never understand His ways. God's works are great and marvelous, and His ways are just and true. There is no complaint here about the way God permitted these people to suffer! It would save us a great deal of sorrow if we would acknowledge God's sovereignty in this same way today! "The Lord is righteous in all His ways, and holy in all His works" (Ps. 145:17).

The phrase "king of saints" can also be read "king of ages." God is the eternal King, but He is also in charge of history. Nothing happens by accident. The singers seek to glorify God and honor Him, the very praise the first angel proclaimed in Revelation 14:7. Antecedents of this song may be found in Psalms 86:9; 90:1-2; 92:5; 98:2; 111:9; and 145:17.

Revelation 15:4 is another anticipation of the kingdom, foretelling the time when all nations shall worship the Lamb and obey Him. This verse also announces that God's judgments are about to be manifested.

The Voice of Fulfillment (Rev. 15:5—16:21)

The "great voice" out of the temple commands the seven angels to pour out the contents of their vials (16:1), after which he announces "It is done!" (16:17) The "mystery of God" is finished! (10:7) The martyrs in glory had asked, "How long?" (6:9-11) and now their cry would be answered.

The seven angels emerge from the heavenly temple (see 11:19), because their work is holy as are the judgments they bring. The angels' clothing reminds us of the priestly garments, for their service is a divine ministry. When the Old Testament tabernacle and temple were dedicated, these earthly buildings were filled with God's glory (Ex. 40:34-35; 2 Chron. 7:1-4); but now the *heavenly* temple is filled with smoke (see Isa. 6:4; Ezek. 10:4). This smoke likewise is evidence of God's glory and power.

Each of the angels has a specific "target" for the contents of his vial. The earth-dwellers have already suffered from the seal and trumpet judgments, but this final series of judgments will climax God's plan, leading to Babylon's fall and Jesus Christ's return to earth.

GRIEVOUS SORES (16:2). This vial judgment reminds us of the sixth plague in Egypt (Ex. 9:8-12; note also Deut. 28:27, 35). Only those who have submitted to "the beast" and who have rejected the warning of the first angel will experience this judgment (Rev. 14:6-7).

Verses 10-11 suggest that these sores do not disappear; for by the time of the fifth vial, people are still in pain from the first judgment. Yet their pain will not cause them to repent (see 9:20-21). William R. Newell used to say, "If men are not won by grace, they will never be won."

It is an awesome thought to consider almost the entire population of the world suffering from a painful malady that nothing can cure. Constant pain affects a person's disposition so that he finds it difficult to get along with other people. Human relations during that period will certainly be at their worst.

WATERS TURNED TO BLOOD (16:3-6). The second and third vials parallel the first plague in Egypt (Ex. 7:14-25). The second vial will center on the sea, and the third will turn the inland waters (rivers and fountains) into blood. When the second trumpet judgment occurred, a third part of the sea became blood; but with this judgment, the entire system of seas and oceans will be polluted. The third trumpet made a third part of the inland waters bitter as wormwood; but the third vial will turn all of those bitter waters into blood.

Heaven gives justification for this terrible judgment: the earth-dwellers have shed the blood of God's people, so it is only right that they should drink blood. In God's government, the punishment fits the crime. Pharaoh tried to drown the Jewish boy babies, but it was his own army that eventually drowned in the Red Sea. Haman planned to hang Mordecai on the gallows and to exterminate the Jews; but he himself was hanged on the gallows, and his family was exterminated (Es. 7:10; 9:10). King Saul refused to obey God and slay the Amalekites, so he was slain by an Amalekite (2 Sam. 1:1-16).

GREAT HEAT FROM THE SUN (16:8-9). All earthly life depends on the light of the sun. In previous judgments, a part of the sun had been dimmed (8:12), but now the heat of the sun is increased. Anyone who has been on the desert knows how merciless the sun's heat can be. Remembering too that the water system is now useless, you can imagine how people will suffer from thirst. Alas, even this judgment will not bring men to their knees! (See Mal. 4:1.)

DARKNESS (16:10-11). This is not worldwide darkness; only "the beast," his throne, and his kingdom are affected. This reminds us of the fifth trumpet (Rev. 9:2) and the ninth plague (Ex. 10:21-23). Where is the throne of "the beast"? His image is in the temple in Jerusalem, so that may be the center of his operation. Or perhaps he is ruling from Rome, in cooperation with the apostate church headquartered there.

When God sent the ninth plague to Egypt, the entire land was dark, except for Goshen where the Israelites lived. The judgment of the fifth vial is just the opposite: there is light for the world, but darkness reigns at the headquarters of "the beast"! Certainly this will be a great blow to his "image" throughout the earth.

THE EUPHRATES DRIED UP (16:12-16). This famous river was mentioned earlier in Revelation, when the sixth trumpet sounded (Rev. 9:13ff) and the angels were loosed who were bound therein. At that time, an army of demonic horsemen was also released. Now, an army from the nations of the world gathers for the great battle at Armageddon. The drying up of the river will make it possible for the army of the "kings of the East" to come to Palestine and invade the Holy Land.

We often speak of "the battle of Armageddon," but nowhere does the Bible use that phrase. On September 2, 1945, when General Douglas MacArthur supervised signing the peace treaty with Japan, he said: "We have had our last chance. If we will not devise something greater and more equitable [than war], Armageddon will be at our door."

The name *Armageddon* comes from two Hebrew words, *har Megiddo*, the hill of Megiddo. The word *Megiddo* means "place of troops" or "place of slaughter." It is also called the Plain of Esdraelon and the Valley of Jezreel. The area is about fourteen miles wide and twenty miles long, and forms what Napoleon called "the most natural battlefield of the whole earth." Standing on Mount Carmel and overlooking that great plain, you can well understand why it would be used for gathering the armies of the nations.

It was on this plain that Barak defeated the armies of Canaan (Jud. 5:19). Gideon met the Midianites there (Jud. 7) and it was there that King Saul lost his life (1 Sam. 31). Titus and the Roman army used this natural corridor, as did the Crusaders in the Middle Ages. British General Allenby used it when he defeated the Turkish armies in 1917.

From a human viewpoint, it appears that the armies of the nations are gathering on their own; but John makes it clear that the military movement is according to God's plan. The satanic trinity, through demonic powers, will influence the nations and cause the rulers to assemble their armies. They will even work miracles that will impress the rulers and cause them to cooperate. But all this will merely fulfill the will of God and accomplish His purposes (see Rev. 17:17). The Gentile nations will look on Armageddon as a battle, but to God, it will be only a "supper" for the fowls of the air (19:17-21).

Zechariah 12 and 14 describe this event from Israel's point of view. Since "the beast" has set up his image in the temple at Jerusalem, and since many of the Jews will not bow down to him, it is natural that the Holy City should be the object of attack. However, not only the Jews are involved; for God has a purpose for the Gentile nations as well. Joel 3:9-21 parallels the Zechariah references, and verse 19 makes clear that God will punish the Gentiles for the way they have treated the Jews. (See also Zeph. 3:8ff; Isa. 24.)

The outcome of the "battle" is recorded in Revelation 19: the Lord returns and defeats His enemies. Obviously, the assembling and marching armies create no problem for Almighty God. When the nations rage and defy Him, "He that sitteth in the heavens shall laugh: the Lord shall have them in derision. Then shall He speak unto them in His wrath, and vex them in His sore displeasure" (Ps. 2:4-5).

"IT IS DONE!" (16:17-21) The devil is "the prince of the power of the air," so perhaps this seventh vial has a special effect on his dominion (Eph. 2:2). But the immediate result is a devastating earthquake that affects the cities of the nations. Satan's entire system is now about to be judged by God: his religious system (the harlot, Rev. 17), his political and economic system (Babylon, Rev. 18), and his military system (the armies, Rev. 19).

The "great city" (16:19) is probably Jerusalem (see 11:8). The Prophet Zechariah prophesied an earthquake that would change the topography of Jerusalem (Zech. 14:4). But the key idea here is that Babylon would fall (see Jer. 50—51). "The beast's" great economic system, which subjugated the people of the world, would be completely destroyed by God.

Added to the earthquake will be a hailstorm with hailstones of tremendous weight. (A talent of silver weighs about 125 pounds!) This judgment is reminiscent of the seventh plague in Egypt (Ex. 9:22-26). Just as Pharaoh and the Egyptian leaders did not repent, so the earth-dwellers will not repent; in fact, they will blaspheme God! No wonder the hail comes, for blasphemers are supposed to be stoned to death (Lev. 24:16).

Reviewing these three chapters, we see the encouragement they give to suffering Christians. The sealed 144,000 will arrive on Mount Zion and praise God (Rev. 14:1-5). The martyrs will also be in glory, praising God (15:1-4). John's message is clear: it is possible to be victorious over "the beast" and be an overcomer!

Movements of armies, confederations of nations, and worldwide opposition to God cannot hinder the Lord from fulfilling His Word and achieving His purposes. Men think they are free to do as they please, but in reality, they are accomplishing the plans and purposes of God!

Every generation of Christians has been able to identify with the events in Revelation 14—16. There has always been a "beast" to oppress God's people and a false prophet to try to lead them astray. We have always been on the verge of an "Armageddon" as the nations wage war.

But in the last days, these events will accelerate and the Bible's prophecies will be ultimately fulfilled. I believe the church will not be on the scene at that time, but both Jewish and Gentile believers will be living who will have to endure Antichrist's rule.

The admonition in Revelation 16:15 applies to us all: "Behold, I [Jesus] come as a thief. Blessed is he that watcheth, and keepeth his garments, lest he walk naked, and they see his shame." Jesus Christ may return at any time, and it behooves us to keep our lives clean, to watch, and to be faithful.

10

Desolation and Destruction!

Revelation 17—18

Beginning in Revelation 17, John describes the Lamb's step-by-step victory over "the beast" and his kingdom. In chapter 17, the religious system is judged; in chapter 18, the political and economic system fall victim. Finally, the Lord Himself returns to earth; judges Satan, "the beast," and the false prophet (19:19-20); and then establishes His kingdom.

One reason John used symbolism was so that his message would encourage believers in any period of church history. The true church is a pure virgin (Rev. 19:7-8; see also 2 Cor. 11:2), but the false religious system is a "harlot" who has abandoned the truth and prostituted herself for personal gain. In every age, there has been a "harlot" who has persecuted God's people; and this will culminate in the last days in a worldwide apostate religious system.

Likewise, every age has featured a "Babylon," a political and economic system that has sought to control people's minds and destinies. Just as the contrast to the "harlot" is the pure bride, so the contrast to "Babylon" is the City of God, the new Jerusalem, the eternal home prepared for the Lamb's wife (Rev. 21:9ff). Each generation of believers must keep itself pure from the pollution of both the "harlot" and "Babylon."

In these two chapters, John prophesies two divine judgments.

The Desolation of the Harlot (Rev. 17)

The scene begins with *an invitation* (17:1-2). One of the angels asks John to come and see what God will do with "the beast's" worldwide religious system. Four times in this chapter, the woman is called a "harlot" (vv. 1, 5, 15-16); and her sin is called "fornication" (vv. 2, 4). Her evil influence has extended to the whole world, reaching even into high places ("the kings of the earth").

Following the invitation, John was carried away "in the Spirit" into the wilderness. There he saw "the harlot" and wrote down *the description* of what he saw (vv. 3-6). Genesis 2 speaks of a pure bride in a lovely garden; but by the Bible's end, civilization has degenerated to an impure harlot in a wilderness! That is what sin does to the world.

The description is very full. The woman is dressed in expensive garments, decorated with gold and precious stones. She is holding a golden cup in her hand and is drunk with the blood of the saints. On her forehead (see 13:16; 14:1) she wears a special name.

Her posture is important. She is seated upon "many waters" (17:1), and upon a scarlet beast with seven heads and ten horns. No wonder John was "greatly astonished" (NIV) when he beheld the woman and "the beast."

But what did it all mean? Thankfully, the angel gave John (and all believers) *the explanation* of these symbols (vv. 7-18).

Let's begin with *the woman.* Verse 18 makes clear that she is identified with a city that existed in John's day ("reigns" is present tense). This city is prosperous and powerful, but also idolatrous ("blasphemy") and dangerous. For one thing, it pollutes the nations with its filth and abomination (pictured by the golden wine cup); for another, it persecutes those who belong to the Lord (v. 6). Power, wealth, pollution, persecution: these words summarize the "great harlot's" involvement on a worldwide scale.

The woman's name also involves "mystery" (v. 5). In the New Testament, a "mystery" is a hidden truth that only the spiritually initiated can understand. To grasp one of God's mysteries requires spiritual intelligence and discernment. In this case, the mystery has to do with Babylon.

The city of Babylon was founded by Nimrod (Gen. 10:8-11). The name *Bab-el* means "the gate of God." Ironically, the famous tower of Babel (11:1-9) was an idolatrous attempt by man to defy God. When the Lord sent judgment on the builders by making mankind's one language into many, the word *bab-el* came to mean "confusion." Later in history, Babylon became a great empire before finally falling to Media-Persia. But from the beginning of Nimrod's city in Genesis 10, an insidious anti-God "Babylonian influence" has been felt throughout history.

The woman is "the great harlot," but she is also "the mother of harlots." The Babylonian system has, in one way or another, given birth to all false religions. She has also seduced men into opposing God and persecuting His servants.

The seven mountains (Rev. 17:9) probably symbolize the city of Rome, built on seven hills. Certainly in John's day, the Roman Empire was living in luxury, spreading false religion, polluting the nations with its idolatry and sin, and persecuting the church.

John's readers would not be surprised when he used an evil harlot to symbolize a wicked city or political system. God even called Jerusalem a harlot! (Isa. 1:21) Isaiah said that Tyre was a harlot (Isa. 23:16-17), and Nahum used this same designation for Nineveh (Nahum 3:4). (Read Jer. 50—51 for further historical parallels to John's prophetic message.)

As noted earlier, scarlet is the color of Satan (Rev. 12:3) and of sin (Isa. 1:18). Scarlet was a popular color in Rome, and both scarlet and purple were associated with rank and riches.

But the woman must not be separated from "the beast" that carries her. "The beast" has seven heads and ten horns. The seven heads symbolize seven mountains (Rev. 17:9) and also seven kings or kingdoms (17:10), in keeping with Old Testament imagery (Ps. 30:7; Dan. 2:35). I have already suggested that the seven mountains can be interpreted geographically as the seven hills of Rome, but they may also be interpreted historically as seven kingdoms.

According to Revelation 17:10, five of these kings (or kingdoms) had passed off the scene, one was present in John's day, and one was yet to come. If so, then the five *past* kingdoms would be Egypt, Assyria, Babylon, Persia, and Greece. The *present* kingdom would be Rome, and the *future* kingdom would be that of "the beast." In order to understand verses 10-11, we must consider verse 12.

"The beast" not only has seven heads, but also ten horns, which represent ten kings. But these are very special kings: they enable "the beast" to rise to power and are even willing to yield their authority to him. Recall that at the opening of the first seal (Rev. 6:1-2), Antichrist began his "peaceful" conquest of the nations. He organized a "United States of Europe," brought peace to the Middle East, and appeared to be the great leader the troubled world was seeking.

But in the midst of the seven-year period, this ruler broke his covenant with Israel (Dan. 9:27) and began to persecute the people of God as well as the nation Israel. Energized by Satan and assisted by the false prophet, "the beast" became the world's dictator and its god. In this way, "the beast" was both "one of the seven [kings, kingdoms]" but also "the eighth." His kingdom was nothing but a revival of the Roman Empire ("one of the seven"), but it was a new kingdom ("the eighth").

But how does all this relate to Babylon? The "Babylonian system" of false religion has been a part of history since Nimrod founded his empire. Scholars have discovered it is amazingly like the true Christian faith! Alas, it is Satan's counterfeit of God's truth. Babylonians practiced the worship of mother and child, and even believed in the death and resurrection of the son.

Readers in John's day would identify "the harlot" with the Roman Empire. Readers in the Middle Ages might identify it as the Roman ecclesiastical system. Today, some believers see "the harlot" and the Babylonian system in an apostate "world church" that minimizes doctrinal truth, rejects the authority of the Word, and tries to unite professed believers on some other basis than faith in Jesus Christ.

However, in the days when John's prophecy will be fulfilled, an amazing thing will happen: "the harlot" will be made desolate by the very system that carried her! It is important to note that *"the beast" carries "the harlot."* Satan (and Antichrist) will use the apostate religious system to accomplish his own ends (i.e., attain world power); but then he will do away with "the harlot" and establish his own religious system. And all of this will be the fulfillment of God's Word! (Rev. 17:17)

Since "the beast" sets up his image in the temple about the middle of the Tribulation, we can assume that "the harlot" and "the beast" work together during those first three and a half years. This is corroborated by the fact that the ten kings assist him in desolating "the harlot" (17:16). These are the same ten kings associated with "the beast" when he sets up the "United States of Europe" during the first half of the Tribulation.

Throughout history, political systems have "used" religious bodies to further their political causes. At the same time, church history reveals that religious groups have used politics to achieve their purposes. The marriage of church and state is not a happy one, and has often spawned children that have created serious problems. When dictators are friendly with religion, it is usually a sign that they want to make use of religion's influence and then destroy it. The church of Jesus Christ has been most influential in the world when it has maintained a separated position.

Compare the description of "the harlot's" desolation with

that of the death of Jezebel (2 Kings 9:30-37).

Finally, note that those who trust the Lord are not influenced by "the harlot" or defeated by the kings (Rev. 17:14). Once again, John points out that the true believers are the "overcomers."

Satan's counterfeit religion is subtle, requiring spiritual discernment to recognize. It was Paul's great concern that the local churches he founded not be seduced away from their sincere devotion to Christ (2 Cor. 11:1-4). In every age, there is the tremendous pressure to conform to "popular religion" and to abandon the fundamentals of the faith. In these last days, we all need to heed the admonitions in 1 Timothy 4 and 2 Timothy 3 and remain true to our Lord.

The Destruction of Babylon (Rev. 18)

Babylon was not only an ancient city and a powerful empire, but also the symbol of mankind's rebellion against God. In Revelation 18, Babylon represents the world system of "the beast," particularly in its economic and political aspects. At the same time, John calls Babylon a "city" at least eight times (14:8; 17:18; 18:10, 16, 18-21). Old Testament prophecy seems to make clear that the city itself will not be rebuilt (Isa. 13:19-22; Jer. 51:24-26, 61-64). Some equate Babylon with Rome, particularly since "the harlot" and "the beast" cooperate during the first half of the Tribulation. Perhaps Peter was using *Babylon* as a "code name" for Rome when he wrote his first letter (1 Peter 5:13). Certainly, John's readers would think of the Roman Empire as they read these words about Babylon.

John heard four voices give four important announcements.

THE VOICE OF CONDEMNATION (18:1-3). This announcement was anticipated in Revelation 14:8 (some commentators would also include 16:19, but I have interpreted the "great city" in that context as Jerusalem). There is a definite reference here to Jeremiah 51—52, where the prophet saw the fall of historical Babylon. But here John saw the destruction of spiritual Babylon, the world system organized by "the beast." It was no ordinary angel that made this announcement, for he had great power and a glory that radiated throughout the whole earth. Despite Satan's devices and the opposition of evil men, "the earth shall be filled with the knowledge of the glory of the Lord" (Hab. 2:14).

The phrase "is fallen, is fallen" not only adds dramatic effect to the announcement, but suggests a dual judgment: ecclesiastical Babylon, "the harlot," in Revelation 17, and political Babylon here in Revelation 18. This thought is amplified in verse 6 when God announces that Babylon will receive "double" for her many sins.

The church, the bride of the Lamb, is the habitation of God (Eph. 2:22); Babylon, on the other hand, is the habitation of Satan (Rev. 18:2). This parallels the judgment on ancient Babylon (Isa. 13:21ff; Jer. 51:37ff). Furthermore, John called the city "a cage of every unclean and hateful bird" (Rev. 18:2). In Christ's Parable of the Sower, He also used the birds as a picture of Satan (Matt. 13:31-32).

This judgment has come because the Babylonian "system" has polluted the whole world. As in the judgment of "the harlot," the sin is that of "fornication" or idolatry. The system intoxicated the people of the world with all the riches and pleasures it had to offer. It catered to those who were "lovers of pleasures more than lovers of God" (2 Tim. 3:4).

Christians in every age have had to heed the warning of 1 John 2:15-17. How easy it is to become fascinated by the things the world has to offer. Like a person taking a sip of wine, we can soon find ourselves drinking deeply and then wanting more. The world system that opposes Christ has always been with us, and we must beware of its subtle influence.

The world system satisfies the desires of the earth-dwellers who follow "the beast" and reject the Lamb. But worldly things never permanently satisfy or last. The love of pleasures and possessions is but an insidious form of idolatry, demonic in its origin and destructive in its outcome.

THE VOICE OF SEPARATION (18:4-8). This admonition parallels Jeremiah 50:8 and 51:6, 45. In all ages, God's true people have had to separate themselves from that which is worldly and anti-God. When God called Abraham, He ordered him to get out of his country (Gen. 12:1). God separated the Jewish nation from Egypt and warned the Israelites not to go back. The church today is commanded to separate itself from that which is ungodly (Rom. 16:17-18; 2 Cor. 6:14—7:1).

John offered two reasons for God's people separating themselves from the diabolical system. The first is that they might avoid pollution, becoming "partakers of her sins" (Rev. 18:4). "Neither be partaker of other men's sins" (1 Tim. 5:22). The word means "joint fellowship or partnership." There is a *good* partnership in the Lord (Phil. 4:14), but there is also an evil partnership that we must avoid (Eph. 5:11). True unity of the Spirit exists among believers, but we must not compromise by joining forces with that which is opposed to Christ.

The second reason is that God's people might be spared the terrible plagues He will send on Babylon. God had patiently endured the growing sins of the evil system, but now the time had come for His wrath to be poured out. He would treat Babylon just as she treated His people.

What specific sins would God judge? We have already noted Babylon's evil influence on the nations of the world, seducing them with *idolatry.* Another sin that will be judged is *pride:* "She hath glorified herself!" (Rev. 18:7) She saw herself as a queen who could never be dethroned, and this false confidence and pride could never be accepted by the Lord. (See Isa. 47 for the parallel, especially vv. 7-9.)

A third sin is Babylon's *worship of pleasures and luxury.* To "live deliciously" (Rev. 18:7) is to live proudly in luxury while others go without. It means to make possessions and pleasures the most important things in life, and to ignore the needs of others. John summarized this attitude as "the lust of the flesh, and the lust of the eyes, and the pride of life" (1 John 2:16).

God's people must not delay in separating themselves from this evil system, because God's judgment will come suddenly and Babylon will be destroyed in a single day. Sometimes God's judgments work silently "as a moth" (Hosea 5:12), but at other times they are "as a lion" (5:14) and spring suddenly, and there is no escape. In one day, the entire economic empire will collapse! But those who have their citizenship in heaven will rejoice at the judgment of God.

THE VOICE OF LAMENTATION (18:9-19). This long paragraph describes the mourning of the merchants as they see Babylon go up in smoke and all their wealth destroyed. The image here is that of a prosperous ancient city that is visited by many ships. The wealth of the city provides for many nations and employs many people. It is worth noting that not only do the merchants lament the fall of Babylon (v. 11), but also the kings of the earth (v. 9). Business and government are so intertwined that what affects one affects the other.

Certainly, the city of Rome was the center for world trade and government in John's day, and it was known for its extravagance and luxury. Politically and economically, the people in the Empire were dependent on Rome. Today, with the complex connections that exist between governments and businesses, and with the interrelated computer systems, it would not take long for "Babylon" to collapse and the world's economic system to be destroyed.

The word translated *wail* (v. 9) means "a loud lamentation" as opposed to silent weeping. In fact, the same word is translated *weep* in verse 11. Note that the merchants are not feeling sorry for the city, but for themselves: they have lost valuable customers! God had brought an end to their life of luxury and wealth. Even their employees weep (vv. 17-18).

John gave an inventory of some of the commodities that brought wealth to these kings, merchants, and shipmasters. Gold, silver, and precious stones led the list. Then he described costly garments (see also v. 16) and items made of different materials. "Thyine wood" (v. 12) was valued highly by the Romans who used it for decorative cabinets and other luxury furnishings.

Imported spices were greatly sought in that day, both for foods and for personal use as perfumes. The city of Rome had to depend on imported foods, just as many nations do today. In fact, our great cities would starve were it not for trucks and trains that daily bring in fresh produce and meats.

Last on the list, and most disturbing, is "slaves and the souls of men" (v. 13). It has been estimated that one third of Rome's population was enslaved; and it was not unusual for 10,000 human beings to be auctioned off *in one day* in the great slave markets of the Empire. There were probably over fifty million slaves throughout the Empire, people who were treated like pieces of furniture, bought and sold, used and abused.

Is John suggesting that there will, in the end times, be a return to slavery? Perhaps not in the ancient sense, but certainly we can see an increasing loss of freedom in our world today. Persons are "bought and sold" (and even traded!) by athletic teams; and our great corporations more and more seek to control the lives of their officers and workers. As people become more enslaved to luxury, with more bills to pay, they find themselves unable to break loose from the "system."

It would take little imagination to conceive of a universal enslavement under the rule of "the beast." We have already seen that he required his mark on everyone that would buy or sell (13:16-17), and he also demanded that all people worship his image. He will promise "freedom," but put men and women in bondage (2 Peter 2:19). He will take advantage of the people's appetites (Rev. 18:14) and use their appetites to enslave them.

John may also have had in mind Ezekiel 27, the lament over the fall of Tyre. As you read that chapter, you will find a number of parallels.

THE VOICE OF CELEBRATION (18:20-24). In contrast to the lament of the kings and merchants is the rejoicing of heaven's inhabitants that Babylon has fallen. How important it is that God's people look at events from God's point of view. In fact, we are commanded to rejoice at the overthrow of Babylon, because in this judgment God will vindicate His servants who were martyred (see Rev. 6:9-11).

Note the repeated refrain, "No more!" Jeremiah used a similar approach when he warned Judah of the nation's coming judgment at the hands of the Babylonians (Jer. 25:8-10). Now that same judgment comes to Babylon herself! This description of Babylon's losses indicates to us that both the luxuries *and* the necessities will be removed. Both music and manufacturing, work and weddings, will come to a violent end.

Revelation 18:24 should be compared with 17:6 and Matthew 23:35. Satan has used religion and business to persecute and slay the people of God. During the first half of the Tribulation, as "the beast" rises to power, ecclesiastical and political-economic Babylon will work together in opposing the Lord and His people. It will seem that God does not care; but at the right time, the Lord will vindicate His people and destroy both "the harlot" and the great city. God is patient with His enemies; but when He does begin to work, He acts suddenly and thoroughly.

We must not think that this voice of celebration calls us to be glad because sinners are judged. The fact of divine judgment ought always to break our hearts, knowing that lost sinners are condemned to eternal punishment. The joy in this section centers on God's righteous judgment, the fact that justice has been done. It is easy for comfortable Bible students to discuss these things in their homes. If you and I were with John on Patmos, or with the suffering saints to whom he wrote, we might have a different perspective. We must never cultivate personal revenge (Rom. 12:17-21), but we must rejoice at the righteous judgments of God.

At this point in our study, the political and economic

system of "the beast" has at last been destroyed. All that remains is for Jesus Christ to come from heaven and personally meet and defeat "the beast" and his armies. This He will do, and then establish His righteous kingdom on earth.

But the important question for you and me is: "Are we citizens of 'Babylon' or citizens of heaven?"

Can you rejoice because your name is written in heaven? If not, then the time has come for you to trust Jesus Christ and "get out of Babylon" and into the family of God.

The King and His Kingdom

Revelation 19—20

"How will it all end?" has been mankind's major question for centuries. Historians have studied the past, hoping to find a clue to understanding the future. Philosophers have tried to penetrate the meaning of things, but they have yet to find the key. No wonder perplexed people have turned in desperation to astrology and spiritism!

The prophetic Word of God shines like a "light . . . in a dark place" (2 Peter 1:19), and on that we can depend. Here in Revelation 19—20, John has recorded five key events that will take place before God "wraps up" human history and ushers in His new heavens and earth.

Heaven Will Rejoice (Rev. 19:1-10)

When Babylon fell on the earth, the command was given in heaven, "Rejoice over her!" (18:20); and what we read in this section is heaven's response to that command. The word *alleuia* is the Greek form of the Hebrew word *hallelujah*, which means "praise the Lord." This is heaven's "Hallelujah Chorus" and it will be sung for three reasons. First . . .

GOD HAS JUDGED HIS ENEMIES (19:1-4). Since the "great whore [harlot]" of Revelation 17 was destroyed by "the beast" and his fellow rulers (17:16) in the middle of the

Tribulation, the "great whore" referred to here must be Babylon the Great. Comparing Revelation 17:2 with 18:3 and 9, the connection is obvious. Both the apostate religious system and the satanic economic-political system led the world astray and polluted mankind. Both were guilty of persecuting God's people and martyring many of them.

The song emphasizes God's attributes, which is the proper way to honor Him. We do not rejoice at the sinfulness of Babylon, or even the greatness of Babylon's fall. We rejoice that God is "true and righteous" (15:3; 16:7; 17:6) and that He is glorified by His holy judgments. As we discovered in Revelation 8:1-6, God's throne and altar are related to His judgments. Verse 3 should be compared with Revelation 14:10-11, and verse 4 with Revelation 5:6-10. Second . . .

GOD IS REIGNING (19:5-6). The literal translation is, "The Lord God omnipotent has begun to reign." This does not suggest that heaven's throne has been empty or inactive, because that is not the case. The Book of Revelation is the "book of the throne," and the omnipotent God has indeed been accomplishing His purposes on earth. This burst of praise is an echo of Psalm 97:1—"The Lord reigneth; let the earth rejoice!"

God has been reigning on the throne of heaven, but He is now about to conquer the thrones of earth as well as the kingdom of Satan and "the beast." In His sovereignty, He has permitted evil men and evil angels to do their worst; but now the time has come for God's will to be done on earth as it is in heaven. Domitian was emperor of Rome when John was on Patmos, and one of his assumed titles was "Lord and God." How significant it must have been, then, to John's readers that he used the word *alleluia* four times in the first six verses of this chapter—truly, only Jehovah is worthy of worship and praise. Third . . .

THE BRIDE IS READY (19:7-10). The bride, of course, is the church (Eph. 5:22-33; 2 Cor. 11:2); and Jesus Christ, the Lamb, is the bridegroom (John 3:29). At a wedding, it is customary to focus attention on the bride; but in this case, it is the *bridegroom* who receives the honor! "Let us be glad and rejoice, and give honor to him."

"What did the bride wear?" is the usual question asked after a wedding. The Lamb's bride is dressed "in the righteous acts of the saints" (literal translation). When the bride arrived in heaven at the Judgment Seat of Christ, she was not at all beautiful (in fact, she was covered with spots, wrinkles, and blemishes according to Paul in Eph. 5:27); but now she is radiant in her glory. She has "made herself ready" for the public ceremony.

Jewish weddings in that day were quite unlike weddings in the Western world. First, there was an engagement, usually made by the parents when the prospective bride and groom were quite young. This engagement was binding and could be broken only by a form of divorce. Any unfaithfulness during the engagement was considered adultery.

When the public ceremony was to be enacted, the groom would go to the bride's house and claim her for himself. He would take her to his home for the wedding supper, and all the guests would join the happy couple. This feast could last as long as a week.

Today, the church is "engaged" to Jesus Christ; and we love Him even though we have not seen Him (1 Peter 1:8). One day, He will return and take His bride to heaven (John 14:1-6; 1 Thes. 4:13-18). At the Judgment Seat of Christ, her works will be judged and all her spots and blemishes removed. This being completed, the church will be ready to return to earth with her Bridegroom at the close of the Tribulation to reign with Him in glory (see Luke 13:29; Matt. 8:11). Some students believe that the entire Kingdom Age will be the "marriage supper."

Revelation 19:9 contains the fourth of the seven "beatitudes" found in the book (see 1:3). Certainly the bride is not invited to her own wedding! This invitation goes out to the guests, believers from the Old Testament era and the Tribulation. During the eternal state, no distinctions will be made among the people of God; but in the Kingdom Age, differences will still exist as the church reigns with Christ and as Israel enjoys the promised messianic blessings.

John was so overwhelmed by all of this that he fell down to worship the angel who was guiding him, an act that he later repeats! (22:8-9) Of course, worshiping angels is wrong (Col. 2:18) and John knew this. We must take into account the tremendous emotional content of John's experience. Like John himself, this angel was only a servant of God (Heb. 1:14); and we do not worship servants. (See Acts 10:25-26.)

Christ Will Return (Rev. 19:11—20:3)

First, John described the Conqueror (Rev. 19:11-16) and then His conquests (19:17—20:3). The rider on the white horse (6:2) is the false Christ, but this rider is the true Christ. He is not coming *in the air* to take His people home (1 Thes. 4:13-18), but *to the earth* with His people, to conquer His enemies and establish His kingdom.

Note the emphasis on Jesus' names (Rev. 19:11-13, 16). He is "Faithful and True" (see 3:14), in contrast to "the beast" who was unfaithful (he broke the covenant with Israel) and false (he ruled by means of deception and idolatry). Suffering saints need to be reminded that God is faithful and will not desert them, because His promises are true.

Perhaps the "secret name" (see v. 12) is the same as the "new name" (3:12). Not knowing what this name is, we cannot comment on it; but it is exciting to know that, even in heaven, we shall learn new things about our Lord Jesus!

"The Word of God" is one of the familiar names of our Lord in Scripture (John 1:1-14). Just as we reveal our minds and hearts to others by our words, so the Father reveals Himself to us through His Son, the incarnate Word (14:7-11). A word is made up of letters, and Jesus Christ is "Alpha and Omega" (Rev. 21:6; 22:13). He is the "divine alphabet" of God's revelation to us.

The Word of God is "living and powerful" (Heb. 4:12); what's more, it fulfills His purposes on earth (Rev. 17:17; note also 6:11; 10:7; 15:1). Jehovah Himself says, "I am watching to see that My Word is fulfilled" (Jer. 1:12, NIV). Just as the Word was the Father's agent in creation (John 1:1-3), so the Word is His agent for judgment and consummation.

Christ's most important name is "King of kings, and Lord of lords" (Rev. 19:16). This is His victorious name (17:14), and it brings to mind references such as Daniel 2:47 and Deuteronomy 10:17. Paul used this same title for our Lord Jesus Christ in 1 Timothy 6:15. The title speaks of Christ's sovereignty, for all kings and lords must submit to Him. No matter who was on the throne of the Roman Empire, Jesus Christ was his King and Lord!

The greatness of Christ is seen not only in His names, but also in John's description of the conquering King (Rev. 19:12-16). The eyes "as a flame of fire" symbolize His searching judgment that sees all (1:14). The many crowns (diadems) indicate His magnificent rule and sovereignty. The vesture dipped in blood speaks of judgment and probably relates to Isaiah 63:1-6 and Revelation 14:20, the conquest of His enemies. It is not our Lord's blood that marks His vesture, but that of His foes.

The sharp sword is a symbol of God's Word (Rev. 19:21; see also Heb. 4:12; Eph. 6:17; Rev. 1:16). This is in keeping with the fact that Christ will consume the enemy "with the spirit of His mouth" (2 Thes. 2:8; note also Isa. 11:4). We have met with the "rod of iron" before (Rev. 2:27; 12:5), a symbol of His justice as He rules over the earth. The image of the winepress must be associated with the judgment at Armageddon (14:14-20; see also Isa. 63:1-6).

Jesus is not alone in His conquest, for the armies of heaven ride with Him. Who are they? Certainly the angels are a part of this army (Matt. 25:31; 2 Thes. 1:7); but so are the saints (1 Thes. 3:13; 2 Thes. 1:10). Jude describes the same scene (Jude 14-15). The word *saints* means "holy ones" and could refer to believers or angels.

It will be unnecessary for the army to fight, for Christ Himself will defeat the enemy through three great victories.

HE WILL DEFEAT THE ARMIES OF THE KINGS OF THE EARTH (19:17-19, 21). These warriors have assembled to fight "against the Lord and against His anointed" (Ps. 2:1-3), but their weapons prove futile. The battle turns out to be a slaughter—a "supper" for the scavenger birds! The first half of Revelation 19 describes the marriage supper of the Lamb; the last half describes the "supper of the great God." (See Luke 17:37; Matt. 24:28.)

The word *flesh* occurs six times in this paragraph. While John's immediate reference is to the human body, eaten by the vultures, there is certainly a deeper meaning here: man fails because he is flesh and relies on flesh. The Bible has nothing good to say about fallen human nature. Recall the Lord's words before the Flood: "My spirit shall not always strive with man, for that he also is flesh" (Gen. 6:3). (See also John 3:6; 6:63; Phil. 3:3; Rom. 7:18.) "All flesh is as grass" (1 Peter 1:24) and must be judged.

This is the account of the well-known "battle of Armageddon," which was anticipated earlier (Rev. 14:14-20; 16:13-16). All that our Lord has to do is speak the Word, and "the sword of His mouth" will devour His enemies.

HE WILL DEFEAT "THE BEAST" AND FALSE PROPHET (19:20). Since Satan's "henchmen" are the leaders of the revolt, it is only right that they be captured and confined. They are cast into the lake of fire (see 20:10, 14-15), the final and permanent place of punishment for all who refuse to submit to Jesus Christ. "The beast" and false prophet are the first persons to be cast into hell. Satan will follow 1,000 years later (20:10), to be joined by those whose names are not recorded in the book of life (20:15).

Today, when an unbeliever dies, his spirit goes to a place called *hades*, which means "the unseen world"—that is, the realm of the dead. When believers die, they go immediately into the presence of the Lord (Phil. 1:19-23; 2 Cor. 5:6-8). Hades will one day be emptied of its dead (Rev. 20:13), who will then be cast into hell to join Satan, "the beast," and the false prophet.

SATAN WILL BE DEFEATED (20:1-3). The "bottomless pit" spoken of in verse 1 is not the same as hell; it is the "abyss" that we have met before in our studies (9:1-2, 11; 11:7; 17:8). Satan is not cast into hell immediately, because God still has one more task for him to perform. Rather, Satan is confined in the bottomless pit for 1,000 years. First, Satan was cast out of *heaven* (12:9), and now he is cast out of *earth!*

Some Bible students feel that the "chaining" of Satan took place when Jesus died on the cross and arose from the dead to ascend to heaven. While it is true that Jesus won His decisive victory over Satan at the Cross, the sentence against the devil has not yet been effected. He is a defeated foe, but he is still free to attack God's people and oppose God's work (1 Peter 5:8). I think it was Dr. James M. Gray who suggested that, if Satan is bound today, it must be with a terribly long chain! Paul was sure that Satan was loose (Eph. 6:10ff), and John agreed with him (Rev. 2:13; 3:9).

Having taken care of His enemies, the Lord is now free to establish His righteous kingdom on the earth.

Saints Will Reign (Rev. 20:4-6)
The phrase "thousand years" occurs six times in verses 1-7. This period in history is known as "the Millennium," from two Latin words, *mille* ("thousand") and *annum* ("year")— the 1,000-year kingdom of Christ on earth. At last, Christ and His church will reign over the nations of the earth, and Israel will enjoy the blessings promised by the prophets. (See Isa. 2:1-5; 4:1-6; 11:1-9; 12:1-6; 30:18-26; 35:1-10.)

Is this a literal kingdom on earth, or should these verses be "spiritualized" and applied to the church today? Some interpreters say that the term "a thousand years" is simply a number meaning "ultimate perfection" (10 x 10 x 10 = 1,000). They assert that it is a symbol of Christ's victory and the church's wonderful blessings now that Satan has been defeated and bound. This view is known as *amillennialism*, which means "no millennium"—that is, no literal kingdom.

The problem with this view is that it does not explain why

John introduced the period with a resurrection of the dead. He was certainly not writing about a "spiritual" resurrection, because he even told how these people died! And in Revelation 20:5, John wrote of another literal resurrection. If we are now in the 1,000-year kingdom of victory, when did this resurrection take place? It seems reasonable to assume that John wrote about a literal physical resurrection of the dead, and a literal kingdom on earth.

What is the purpose of the millennial kingdom? For one thing, it will be the fulfillment of God's promises to Israel *and to Christ* (Ps. 2; Luke 1:30-33). Our Lord reaffirmed them to His own apostles (Luke 22:29-30). This kingdom will be a worldwide display of Christ's glory, when all nature will be set free from the bondage of sin (Rom. 8:19-22). It will be the answer to the prayers of the saints, "Thy kingdom come!" It will also be God's final demonstration of the sinfulness of sin and the wickedness of the human heart apart from God's grace, but more on this later.

The Tribulation martyrs will be raised from the dead and given glorious thrones and rewards. The church will share in this reign, as symbolized by the twenty-four elders (Rev. 5:10; see also 2:26-28; 3:12, 21; 1 Thes. 4:13-18; 2 Tim. 2:12). Some Bible students believe that the Old Testament saints will also be a part of this "first resurrection" (Dan. 12:1-4).

The phrase "general resurrection" is not found in the Bible. On the contrary, the Bible teaches *two* resurrections: the first is of the saved and leads to blessing; the second is of all the lost and leads to judgment (note especially John 5:28-29; Dan. 12:2). These two resurrections will be separated by 1,000 years.

Revelation 20:6 describes the special blessings of those who share in the first resurrection. They did not *earn* these blessings; they are part of the believer's inheritance in Jesus Christ. This is the sixth of the seven "beatitudes" in Revelation; the final one is in 22:7. These resurrected believers will share Christ's glorious life, reigning as kings and priests with Him, and never experience the "second death," the lake of fire (hell, 20:14).

During the Millennium, the inhabitants of the earth will include not only glorified saints, but also citizens of the nations who bow in submission to Jesus Christ (see Matt. 25:31-40; also 8:11). Because of the earth's perfect conditions, people will live long lives (Isa. 65:17-25, especially v. 20). They will marry and have children who will outwardly conform to our Lord's righteous rule. But not all of them will be truly born again as the Millennium progresses; and this explains why Satan will be able to gather a great army of rebels at the close of the Kingdom Age (Rev. 20:8).

For many centuries, man has dreamed of a "golden age," a "utopia" in which the human race will be free from war, sickness, and even death. Men have tried to achieve this goal on their own and have failed. It is only when Jesus Christ reigns on David's throne that the kingdom will come and the earth be delivered from the oppression of Satan and sin.

Satan Will Revolt (Rev. 20:7-10)

At the close of the Millennium, Satan will be released from the pit and permitted to lead one last revolt against the Lord. Why? As final proof that the heart of man is desperately wicked and can be changed only by God's grace. Imagine the tragedy of this revolt: people who have been living in a perfect environment, under the perfect government of God's Son, will finally admit the truth and rebel against the King! Their obedience will be seen as mere *feigned* submission, and not true faith in Christ at all.

The naming of "Gog and Magog" (v. 8) does not equate this battle with the one described in Ezekiel 38—39; for that army invades from the north, while this one comes from the four corners of the earth. These two events are related, however, inasmuch as in both battles, Israel is the focal point. In this case, Jerusalem will be the target ("beloved city," Pss. 78:68; 87:2). God will deal with this revolt very quickly and efficiently, and Satan will be cast into hell. Note that "the beast" and false prophet will still be suffering in the lake of fire after 1,000 years! (See Matt. 25:41.)

In one sense, the millennial kingdom will "sum up" all that God has said about the heart of man during the various periods of history. It will be a reign of law, and yet law will not change man's sinful heart. Man will still revolt against God. The Millennium will be a period of peace and perfect environment, a time when disobedience will be judged swiftly and with justice; and yet in the end the subjects of the King will follow Satan and rebel against the Lord. A perfect environment cannot produce a perfect heart.

God is now about to "wrap up" human history. One great event remains.

Sinners Are Recompensed (Rev. 20:11-15)

There shall be a second resurrection, and the unsaved will be raised and will stand before God's judgment. Do not confuse this judgment at the white throne with the Judgment Seat of Christ, where believers will have their works judged and rewarded. At this judgment, there will be only unbelievers; and there will be no rewards. John described here an awesome scene. Heaven and earth will flee away and no place will be left for sinners to hide! All must face the Judge!

The Judge is Jesus Christ, for the Father has committed all judgment to Him (John 5:22-30; Matt. 19:28; Acts 17:31). These lost sinners rejected Christ in life; now they must be judged by Him and face eternal death.

From where do these "dead" come? Death will give up the bodies, and hades (the realm of the spirits of the dead) will give up the spirits. There will even be a resurrection of bodies from the sea. No sinner will escape.

Jesus Christ will judge these unsaved people on the basis of what is written "in the books." What books? For one thing, God's Word will be there. "The Word that I have spoken, the same shall judge him in the last day" (John 12:48). Every sinner will be held accountable for the truth he or she has heard in this life.

There will also be a book containing the works of the

sinners being judged, though this does not suggest that a person can do good works sufficient to enter heaven (Eph. 2:8-9; Titus 3:5). Why, then, will Jesus Christ consider the works, good and bad, of the people before the white throne? To determine the degree of punishment they will endure in hell. All of these people will be cast into hell. Their personal rejection of Jesus Christ has already determined their destiny. But Jesus Christ is a righteous Judge, and He will assign each sinner the place that he deserves.

There are degrees of punishment in hell (Matt. 11:20-24). Each lost sinner will receive just what is due him, and none will be able to argue with the Lord or question His decision. God knows what sinners are doing, and His books will reveal the truth.

"The Book of Life" will be there, containing the names of God's redeemed people (Phil. 4:3; Rev. 21:27; note also 13:8; 17:8). No unsaved person will have his or her name in the Lamb's Book of Life; only true believers are recorded there (Luke 10:20).

When the judgment is finished, all of the lost will be cast into hell, the lake of fire, the second death. Many people reject the biblical doctrine of hell as being "unchristian," and yet Jesus clearly taught its reality (Matt. 18:8; 23:15, 33; 25:46; Mark 9:46). A sentimental kind of humanistic religion will not face the reality of judgment, but teaches a God who loves everyone into heaven and sends no one to hell.

Hell is a witness to the righteous character of God. He must judge sin. Hell is also a witness to man's responsibility, the fact that he is not a robot or a helpless victim, but a creature able to make choices. God does not "send people to hell"; they send themselves by rejecting the Saviour (John 3:16-21; Matt. 25:41). Hell is also a witness to the awfulness of sin. If we once saw sin as God sees it, we would understand why a place such as hell exists.

In light of Calvary, no lost sinner can condemn God for casting him into hell. God has provided a way of escape, patiently waiting for sinners to repent. He will not lower His standards or alter His requirements. He has ordained that faith in His Son is the only way of salvation.

The White Throne Judgment will be nothing like our modern court cases. At the white throne, there will be a Judge but no jury, a prosecution but no defense, a sentence but no appeal. No one will be able to defend himself or accuse God of unrighteousness. What an awesome scene it will be!

Before God can usher in His new heavens and earth, He must finally deal with sin; and this He will do at the Great White Throne.

You can escape this terrible judgment by trusting Jesus Christ as your personal Saviour. By so doing, you never will be a part of the second resurrection or experience the terrors of the second death, the lake of fire.

"He that heareth My Word," said Jesus, "and believeth on Him that sent Me, hath everlasting life, and shall not come into condemnation [judgment], but is passed from death unto life" (John 5:24).

Have you trusted Him and passed from death unto life?

12
All Things New!

Revelation 21—22

Human history begins in a Garden and ends in a City that is like a garden paradise. In the Apostle John's day, Rome was the admired city; yet God compared it to a harlot. "That which is highly esteemed among men is abomination in the sight of God" (Luke 16:15). The eternal city of God is compared to a beautiful bride (Rev. 21:9), because it is the eternal home for God's beloved people.

God's statements recorded in Revelation 21:5-6 aptly summarize these final two chapters: "Behold, I make all things new. . . . It is done!" What began in Genesis is brought to completion in Revelation, as the following summary shows:

Genesis	Revelation
Heavens and earth created, 1:1	New heavens and earth, 21:1
Sun created, 1:16	No need of the sun, 21:23
The night established, 1:5	No night there, 22:5
The seas created, 1:10	No more seas, 21:1
The curse announced, 3:14-17	No more curse, 22:3
Death enters history, 3:19	No more death, 21:4
Man driven from the tree, 3:24	Man restored to paradise, 22:14
Sorrow and pain begin, 3:17	No more tears or pain, 21:4

The Citizens of the City (Rev. 21:1-8)

John gives us a threefold description of the citizens of the city. First . . .

THEY ARE GOD'S PEOPLE (21:1-5). The first heaven and earth were prepared for the first man and woman and their descendants. God had readied everything for them when He placed them in the garden. Unfortunately, our first parents sinned, ushering death and decay into God's beautiful world. Creation is in bondage and travail (Rom. 8:18-23), and even the heavens "are not clean in His sight" (Job 15:15).

God has promised His people a new heaven and earth (Isa. 65:17; 66:22). The old creation must make way for the new creation if God is to be glorified. Jesus called this event "the regeneration" of the earth (Matt. 19:28), and Peter explained it as a cleansing and renewing by fire (2 Peter 3:10-13). Bible students are not agreed as to whether the old elements will be renewed or whether the old will be destroyed and a whole new creation ushered in. The fact that the Greek word translated *new* means "new in character" (Rev. 21:1, 5) may lend credence to the former explanation.

"No more sea" does not mean "no more water." It simply indicates that the new earth will have a different arrangement as far as water is concerned. Three-fourths of our globe consists of water, but this won't be the case in the eternal state. In John's day, the sea meant danger, storms, and separation (John himself was on an island at the time!); so perhaps John was giving us more than a geography lesson.

Even despite Scripture's description, it is difficult to imagine what the eternal city will be like. John characterizes it as a *holy* city (see Rev. 21:27), a *prepared* city (see John 14:1-6), and a *beautiful* city, as beautiful as a bride on her wedding day. He amplifies these characteristics in Revelation 21—22.

But the most important thing about the city is that God dwells there with His people. The Bible gives an interesting record of the dwelling places of God. First, God walked with man in the Garden of Eden. Then He dwelt with Israel in the tabernacle and later the temple. When Israel sinned, God had to depart from those dwellings. Later, Jesus Christ came to earth and "tabernacled" among us (John 1:14). Today, God does not live in man-made temples (Acts 7:48-50), but in the bodies of His people (1 Cor. 6:19-20) and in the church (Eph. 2:21-22).

In both the tabernacle and the temple, the veil stood between men and God. That veil was torn in two when Jesus died, thus opening a "new and living way" for God's people (Heb. 10:19ff). Even though God dwells in believers today by His Spirit, we still have not begun to understand God or fellowship with Him as we would like; but one day, we shall dwell in God's presence and enjoy Him forever.

The eternal city is so wonderful that the best way John found to describe it was by contrast—"no more." The believers who first read this inspired book must have rejoiced to know that, in heaven, there would be no more pain, tears, sorrow, or death; for many of their number had been tortured and slain. In every age, the hope of heaven has encouraged God's people in times of suffering. Second . . .

THE CITIZENS OF HEAVEN ARE A SATISFIED PEOPLE (21:6). People who live in modern cities do not think much about water, but this was a major concern in John's day. No doubt John himself, working in the Roman mines, had known the meaning of thirst. Tortured saints throughout the ages would certainly identify with this wonderful promise from the Lord. Free and abundant living water for all! Third . . .

THESE HEAVENLY CITIZENS ARE AN OVERCOMING PEOPLE (21:7-8). "He that overcometh" is a key phrase in this book (2:7, 11, 17, 26; 3:5, 12, 21; note also 12:11). As John pointed out in his first epistle, all true believers are overcomers (1 John 5:4-5), so this promise is not just for the "spiritually elite." Because we are the children of God, we shall inherit all things.

After the great Chicago fire of 1871, evangelist Dwight L. Moody went back to survey the ruins of his house. A friend came by and said to Moody, "I hear you lost everything."

"Well," said Moody, "you understood wrong. I have a good deal more left than I lost."

"What do you mean?" the inquisitive friend asked. "I didn't know you were that rich."

Moody then opened his Bible and read to him Revelation 21:7—"He that overcometh shall inherit all things, and I will be his God."

In contrast to the overcomers, verse 8 describes the people who *were overcome* by sin and would not trust the Lord. What is their destiny? The lake of fire! The world considers Christians as "losers," but it is the unbelievers who are the losers!

The fearful are the cowardly, the people who did not have the courage to stand up for Christ. (See Matt. 10:32-33.) The word *abominable* means "polluted," and refers to those who indulged in sin and were thus polluted in mind, spirit, and body (2 Cor. 7:1). The other characteristics mentioned in Revelation 21:8 need no special explanation, except to note that all of them would be true of "the beast's" followers (note 17:4, 6; 18:3, 9; 19:2).

The Character of the City (Rev. 21:9—22:5)

The eternal city is not only the home of the bride; it *is* the bride! A city is not buildings; it is people. The city John saw was holy and heavenly; in fact, it descended to earth from heaven, where it was prepared. John's description staggers the imagination, even accepting the fact that a great deal of symbolism is involved. Heaven is a real place of glory and beauty, the perfect home for the Lamb's bride.

We have already noted that "the glory of God" has appeared in different places throughout history. God's glory dwelt in the tabernacle and then in the temple. Today, His glory dwells in believers and in His church. For all eternity, the glory of God will be seen in His holy city. It is the only light the city will need.

The city's description follows the pattern of cities with which John's readers were familiar: foundations, walls, and gates. The foundations speak of *permanence*, in contrast to the tents in which "pilgrims and strangers" lived (Heb. 11:8-10). The walls and gates speak of *protection*. God's people will never have to fear any enemies. Angels at the gates will act as sentries!

In this city, saints of the Old Covenant and the New Covenant will be united. The twelve gates are identified with the twelve tribes of Israel, and the twelve foundations with the twelve apostles (see Eph. 2:20). Including the tribe of Levi, there were actually thirteen tribes; and, including Paul, there were thirteen apostles. When John listed the tribes in Revelation 7, both Dan and Ephraim were omitted, perhaps indicating that we should not press these matters too literally. John is simply assuring us that all of God's believing people will be included in the city (Heb. 11:39-40).

John had measured the earthly Jerusalem (Rev. 11), but now he is invited to measure the heavenly city. *Foursquare* means "equal on all sides," so the city might be a cube or a pyramid. More importantly, the fact that it is equal on all sides indicates the perfection of God's eternal city: nothing is out of order or balance.

The measurements are staggering! If we take a cubit as eighteen inches, then the city walls are 216 feet high! If a furlong is taken as 600 feet (measures differed in ancient days), the city would be about 1,500 miles square! This is about three-fourths the size of the United States. And there will be plenty of room for everyone!

The city's construction cannot but fascinate us. The walls are jasper, which is a clear crystal; but the city itself will be made of pure gold, as clear as crystal. The light of God's glory will shine throughout the city, resembling a huge holy of holies.

Building foundations are usually underground, but these foundations will not only be visible but beautifully garnished with precious stones. Each separate foundation will have its own jewel, and the blending of the colors will be magnificent as God's light shines through.

No one can be dogmatic about the colors of these gems, and it really does not matter. Jasper, as we have seen, is a clear crystal. Sapphire is a blue stone, and chalcedony is probably greenish-blue. The emerald, of course, is green; and the sardonyx is like our onyx, a white stone streaked with brown, though some scholars describe it as red and white.

Sardius is a red stone (sometimes described as "blood red"), and chrysolite a yellow quartz like our modern topaz. Beryl is green and topaz a yellow-green. We are not sure about the chrysoprasus; some think it is a golden-tinted stone, others, an apple-green color. The jacinth is probably blue, though some claim it was yellow; and the amethyst is a rich purple, or blue-red.

Our God is a God of beauty, and He will lavish His beauty on the city He is preparing for His people. Perhaps Peter had the holy city in mind when he wrote about the "manifold grace of God" (1 Peter 4:10), for the word translated *manifold* means "many colored, variegated."

In ancient times, the pearl was considered a "royal gem," produced by a mollusk covering an irritating grain of sand within its shell. But the pearl gates of the heavenly city will never be closed (Rev. 21:25) because there will be no danger of anything entering that would disturb or defile her citizens.

John noted that some items were missing from the city, but their absence only magnified its glory. There will be no temple, since the entire city will be indwelt by God's presence. Indeed, "secular" and "sacred" will be indistinguishable in heaven. The sun and moon will be absent since the Lord is the light of the city, and there will never be any night (see Isa. 60:19).

The mention of nations in Revelation 21:24 and 26 suggests that there will be *peoples* (plural) on the new earth. Since in the eternal state there will be only glorified beings, we must not think that the earth will be populated with various nations such as exist today. Instead, these verses reflect the ancient practice of kings and nations bringing their wealth and glory to the city of the greatest king. In the heavenly city, everyone will honor the "King of kings." (See Pss. 68:29; 72:10-11; Isa. 60.)

In Revelation 22:1-5, we move inside the city to discover that it is like a beautiful garden, reminiscent of the Garden of Eden. There were four rivers in Eden (Gen. 2:10-14), but there is only one river in the heavenly city. Ezekiel saw a purifying river flowing from the temple, certainly a millennial scene (Ezek. 47); but this river will flow directly from God's throne, the very source of all purity. Man was prohibited from eating of the tree of the knowledge of good and evil, and prevented from eating of the tree of life (Gen. 2:15-17; 3:22-24). But in the eternal home, man will have access to the tree of life. The river and the tree symbolize abundant life in the glorious city.

"No more curse" takes us back to Genesis 3:14-19 where the curse began. Interestingly, even the Old Testament closes with the statement, "Lest I come and smite the earth with a curse" (Mal. 4:6). But the New Testament announces, "And there shall be no more curse!" Satan will be consigned to hell; all of creation will be made new; and the curse of sin will be gone forever.

What will we do in heaven for all eternity? Certainly, we shall praise the Lord, but we shall also serve Him. "His servants shall serve Him" (Rev. 22:3) is a great encouragement to us, for in heaven our service will be perfect. As we seek to serve the Lord here on earth, we are constantly handicapped by sin and weakness; but all hindrances will be gone when we get to glory. Perfect service in a perfect environment!

What will this service be? We are not told, nor do we need to know now. It is sufficient that we know what God wants us to do *today*. Our faithfulness in life prepares us for higher service in heaven. In fact, some students think that we shall have access to the vast universe and perhaps be sent on special missions to other places. But it is useless to speculate, because God has not seen fit to fill in the details.

Not only shall we be servants in heaven, but we shall also be kings. We shall reign forever and ever! This speaks of sharing Christ's authority in glory. As believers, we are seated with Christ in the heavenlies today (Eph. 2:1-10); but in the eternal state, we shall reign as kings over the new heavens and earth. What an honor! What grace!

Certainly, many interesting questions could be asked about our future abode in heaven, but most must go unanswered until we reach our glorious home. In fact, John closed his book by reminding us that we have responsibilities today *because* we are going to heaven.

The Challenge of the City (Rev. 22:6-21)

Heaven is more than a destination; it is a motivation. Knowing that we shall dwell in the heavenly city ought to make a difference in our lives here and now. The vision of the heavenly city motivated the patriarchs as they walked with God and served Him (Heb. 11:10, 13-16). Knowing that He was returning to the Father in heaven also encouraged Jesus Christ as He faced the Cross (Heb. 12:2). The assurance of heaven must not lull us into complacency or carelessness, but spur us to fulfill our spiritual duties. First . . .

WE MUST KEEP GOD'S WORD (22:6-11, 18-19). Because what John wrote is the Word of God, his words are faithful and true (see Rev. 19:11). The same God who spoke through the prophets also spoke through the Apostle John. As the "capstone" of God's revelation, John's book cannot be divorced from the rest of the Bible. If we deny that John wrote the truth, then we must also deny the prophets.

What does it mean to "keep the sayings of the prophecy of this book"? (22:7) Basically, it means to guard, to watch over, to preserve intact. We must not add to the Word of God or take anything from it (see Deut. 4:2; Prov. 30:5-6). And this responsibility is especially great in light of Christ's return. The word *shortly* in Revelation 22:6 means "quickly come to pass." The church has expected Christ to return since the days of the apostles, and He has not yet come; but when John's prophecies begin to be fulfilled, they will happen very quickly. There will be no delay.

The warnings in verses 18-19 do not suggest that people who tamper with the Bible will be brought back to earth to suffer the Tribulation's plagues, or that they will lose their salvation. Nobody fully understands the Bible or can explain everything in it; and those of us who teach the Word sometimes have to change our interpretations as we grow in knowledge. God sees the heart, and He can separate ignorance from impudence and immaturity from rebellion.

It was customary in ancient days for writers to put this kind of warning at the close of their books, because the people who copied them for public distribution might be tempted to tamper with the material. However, John's warning was not addressed to a writer, but to the hearer, the believer in the congregation where this book was read aloud. By analogy, however, it would apply to anyone reading and studying the book today. We may not be able to explain the penalties given, but we do know this: it is a dangerous thing to tamper with the Word of God. The one who guards the Word and obeys it will be blessed; the one who alters it will be disciplined in some way.

For a second time, John was overwhelmed by what he saw and heard; and he fell down to worship the angel who was speaking to him (see 19:10). The angel gave John three words of counsel: do not worship angels; worship God; and do not seal up the Revelation. The Prophet Daniel was commanded to seal his book (Dan. 12:4), because the time was not yet ready. John's book was an "apocalypse," an unveiling (Rev. 1:1); and, therefore, it must not be sealed.

Once again, the Holy Spirit is reminding us of the living unity of God's Word. We have seen in our study how John, led by the Spirit, reached back into the Old Testament and used many of the images found there, including Daniel's prophecy. Scripture is its own best interpreter.

Does Revelation 22:11 suggest that God does not want men

to repent and change their ways? No, because that would be contrary to the message of Revelation and of the Gospel itself. The angel's words must be understood in light of the repeated statement, "Behold, I come quickly" (vv. 7, 12), as well as his statement, "For the time is at hand" (v. 10). Jesus Christ's coming will occur so quickly that men will not have time to change their characters.

Verse 11, therefore, is a solemn warning that decision determines character, and character determines destiny. Suffering believers might ask, "Is it worth it to live a godly life?" John's reply is, "Yes! Jesus is returning, and He will reward you!" Next comes John's second admonition.

WE HAVE THE RESPONSIBILITY OF SERVING THE LORD (22:12-15). "My reward is with Me" implies that God is mindful of our sufferings and our service, and nothing will ever be done in vain if it is done for Him. At the Judgment Seat of Christ, believers will be judged according to their works; and rewards will be given to those who have been faithful.

Throughout church history, there have been those who have (to use Dwight L. Moody's words) become "so heavenly minded that they were no earthly good." They quit their jobs, sold their property, and sat and waited for Jesus to return. All of them have been embarrassed, of course, because it is unbiblical to set dates for His coming. It is also unbiblical to become careless and lazy just because we believe Jesus is coming soon. Paul faced this problem with some of the believers in Thessalonica (2 Thes. 3).

No wonder John added, "Blessed are they that do His commandments" (Rev. 22:14). If we really believe that Jesus is coming soon, we will watch and be faithful (Luke 12:35ff).

Revelation 22:13 is a great encouragement to anyone who seeks to serve the Lord. Whatever God starts, He will finish; for He is the Alpha and Omega, the beginning and the ending, the first and the last (see Phil. 1:6; 2:12-13). Our third responsibility . . .

WE MUST KEEP OUR LIVES CLEAN (22:14-16). The contrast here is between those who do God's commandments and enter the city, and those who reject His Word and are excluded from the city (see 21:8, 27). It is not likely that those who "do His commandments" are a special or an elite group of saints. The phrase is similar to "them that overcome" and characterizes all the people of God. Obedience to God's Word is a mark of true salvation.

Our Lord's titles in verse 16 are most interesting. The "root" is buried in the ground where no one can see it, but the "star" is in the heavens where everyone can see it. In "the root and offspring of David" we have Jesus' Jewish, national name, but in "the bright and morning star" we have His universal name. One speaks of humility, the other of majesty and glory.

As "the root . . . of David," Jesus Christ brought David into existence. As "the offspring of David," Jesus came into this world, born a Jew from David's line. Both the deity and the humanity of Jesus are evident here. For a parallel, see Matthew 22:41-46.

The "morning star" announces dawn's soon arrival. Jesus Christ will come for His church as "the morning star." But when He returns to judge, it will be as "the Sun of righteousness" in burning fury (Mal. 4:1-3). Because God's people look for their Lord's return, they keep their lives clean and dedicated to Him (1 John 2:28–3:3). Therefore . . .

WE MUST KEEP EXPECTING JESUS CHRIST TO RETURN (22:17, 20-21). Three times in this closing chapter John wrote, "I [Christ] come quickly" (vv. 7, 12, 20). But He has "delayed" His return for nearly 2,000 years! Yes, He has; and Peter tells us why: God wants to give this sinful world opportunity to repent and be saved (2 Peter 3:1ff). In the meantime, the Spirit of God, through the church (the bride), calls for Jesus to come; for the bride wants to meet her Bridegroom and enter into her home. "Even so, come, Lord Jesus" (Rev. 22:20).

But believers ought also to invite lost sinners to trust Christ and drink the water of life. Indeed, when the church lives in expectancy of Christ's return, such an attitude provokes ministry and evangelism as well as purity of heart. We want to tell others of the grace of God. A true understanding of Bible prophecy should both motivate us to obey God's Word and to share God's invitation with a lost world.

If our study of Revelation has been truly led by the Spirit, then we will join John in the Bible's last prayer:

"Even so, come, Lord Jesus!"

Are you ready?

Chapter One

A Very Special Book
(Revelation 1)

1. What images come to your mind when you think of the Book of Revelation or of the "apocalypse"?

2. Wiersbe writes: "We need to approach this book as wonderers and worshippers, not as academic students." How can we best do that?

3. As you look at the church in the modern world, what evidence do you see that we function with Christ's second coming in mind?

4. Revelation tells us, as Isaiah did, that Jesus Christ is the Alpha and Omega, the beginning and the end. What does that mean in your everyday life?

5. The first church, addressed in Revelation 2, was accused of losing their first love. What kinds of evidence do you see in the Church today that we face a similar scenario?

6. As you read the symbolic description of Christ in the first chapter of Revelation, what is the most striking attribute that you see represented?

7. In what ways do you think God wants us to respond of Revelation?

8. What are some of your hopes and hesitations about Christ's "Second Coming"?

Chapter Two

Christ and the Churches, Part 1
(Revelation 2)

1. Think of a time when you were looking for a new church. What did you use as criteria for determining if that church was a good place for you to serve and worship?

2. The Ephesian church was praised for examining the people who spoke to them to be sure they were genuine. Name some examples of examination that are present in your church today.

3. Evaluate for a moment in your church and in your own life whether your first love is still intact. What are the evidences that Jesus Christ is still our first love?

4. Smyrna was a persecuted church. How do you think your church would stand up today if the members were persecuted for attending? What new things would you learn about your church in that situation?

5. The church at Pergamos was criticized for fraternizing with the enemy, for not keeping themselves separate enough from their idolatrous culture. Where is the balance between keeping ourselves separate from sin and building relationships with sinners?

6. Thyatira was a church that was socially conscious but morally weak. How can we keep from tolerating evil?

7. If there were a section of Revelation 2 written to your church, what would you be praised for? Accused of? Admonished to do?

Chapter Three

Christ and the Churches, Part 2
(Revelation 3)

1. Think of a church you may have known about that was "alive in name only." What were the evidences of their spiritual demise?

2. Vance Havner plotted the stages of a ministry as "a man, a movement, a machine, and then a monument." Give some examples of ministries you have seen in one of these stages.

3. List some reasons people and churches find it easy at times to glory "in past splendor, but ignore present decay."

4. God put an open door of opportunity in front of the church at Philadelphia. What open doors of ministry are before the Church today?

5. We tend to see churches with large congregations as the successful churches with grand opportunities for ministry. Philadelphia, on the other hand, was weak. What are God's standards for using a church or making it successful?

6. The Laodicean church was described as lukewarm. Describe a lukewarm church or organization today.

7. The church at Laodicea was unaware of it's true state of being. What kept it, and what keeps us, unaware of our own shortcomings and needs?

8. We often use Revelation 3:20 in the context of salvation. Even after we are saved, what are other situations in which God stands outside of our lives asking to be more involved?

Chapter Four

Come, Let Us Adore Him!
(Revelation 4-5)

1. What would be your definition of worship?

2. In what kinds of situations do you feel most able to worship?

3. God sitting on His throne gives us the image of His sovereignty, His complete control over the events of our lives. How have you seen God's sovereignty at work in your life?

4. Revelation was written to people who were suffering. How does our suffering affect our worship? How does our worship affect our suffering?

5. Jesus is described as both a lion and a lamb. Considering the traits you know of both animals and what you know of Christ's life, in what ways are these comparisons on target?

6. From the earliest days of the temple in Jerusalem to this prophetic image at the end of time, music has been an essential part of worship. How does music affect your worship?

7. Review the song the elders sang (5:9-13) as they worshiped together. If you were standing before Christ and could praise Him out loud, what would your song include?

8. If you had been John, witnessing this fabulous vision of worship and praise, what words would you have used to describe it?

9. What part of this vision can we carry into our everyday lives to teach us more of how to worship Christ?

Chapter Five

The Seals and the Sealed
(Revelation 6-7)

1. What elements of our society, particularly in regard to celebrities and the media, will make it complex to identify the Antichrist?

2. Describe the strength of conviction it must take to be a martyr, to be willing to die for your faith.

3. Think of a time when you prayed for God's vengeance on a wrong you witnessed. How did God respond to your prayer?

4. Wiersbe says, "Horses represent God's activity on earth, the forces He uses to accomplish His divine purposes." What "horses" do you see expressing His sovereignty in the world around you?

5. John writes in Revelation about the catastrophes associated with the sixth seal. What have been your observations in regard to the spiritual effects on people who endure catastrophes?

6. We often read in the New Testament about the love of Christ. What do you understand from Revelation 6-7 about the justice of Christ?

7. In what ways does the Holy Spirit "seal" us in this life?

8. Think of moments when you have worshiped God with joy and wonder. How do you think that experience will compare with the worship in heaven?

Chapter Six

Blow the Trumpets!
(Revelation 8-9)

1. How would you compare current society to the Pharaoh who said, "Who is the lord that we should serve Him?"

2. Imagine the moments of silence when the seventh seal was opened. What makes silence so powerful when we stand before God?

3. In what ways have you seen prayer help God's will to be done on earth?

4. The "desolation in the seas," the second trumpet judgment, reveals to us how one part of nature can affect everything else on earth. List some elements of nature that we take for granted, but would affect us all if they were altered.

5. List some events that show the evil in our world taking advantage of the darkness, as will happen at the close of the Tribulation when the sun and moon will be darkened.

6. Why do you think locusts were an apt image for demonic beings?

7. Describe the elements of human nature that cause us to remain in our sin in the face of God's judgment?

8. What is your primary feeling as you read about the end of the world?

9. What kinds of idols do you see currently on the rise in our culture?

Chapter Seven

A *Time for Testimony*
(Revelation 10-11)

1. What evidence have you seen of angels in your lifetime?

2. Why do you think John was prohibited from revealing what God thundered?

3. How can we "incarnate" the Word of God for the world around us?

4. What prevents humanity from accepting God's provision for their sin through Christ's death?

5. Think of a time when God's Word was sweet to you and a time when it was bitter. What made the difference?

6. In the first half of the Tribulation two powerful witnesses uphold God's truth to their generation. Who are some powerful witnesses in our present generation who are doing that?

7. In thinking about the martyrdom of the two witnesses, how do you respond to the statement, "Nothing can hurt me until it's my time to go"?

8. As we prepare for the return of Christ and the judgment of the world, how can our lives serve as testimonies for God?

9. The testimony of the elders came through their acts of worship. How does our worship testify to the world around us?

Chapter Eight

The Terrible Trio
(Revelation 12–13)

1. List some historical figures that have used their influence to cause suffering. What are some traits these people had in common?

2. Why do you think God allows evil people and evil nations to prosper?

3. Describe a time in your life where Satan, the devil, acted as an accuser or tried to destroy you.

4. The anti-Christ or beast will be accomplishing the purposes of evil, even though he will be slick and will appear to work under the auspices of peace. List some smaller versions of the beast that we can find in our world today.

5. What makes it easy for the general public to be deceived by celebrities and political figures?

6. The false prophet will lift up the beast in the same way that the Holy Spirit lifts up Christ. What are the ways the Holy Spirit lifts up Christ?

7. If the beast appeared now with miracles and with charisma, how do you think our current society would respond?

8. What is the closest comparison you can make in our current experience to the mark that will be required in order to buy and sell?

9. In what ways is our world already developing the kinds of systems that will support the work of the beast?

Chapter Nine

Voices of Victory
(Revelation 14–16)

1. Think about a sports event or another contest where you felt a tremendous sense of victory. Describe the reactions of that moment.

2. In what ways does it give you strength or encouragement to know that there will be those kinds of experiences in heaven?

3. How do you see the witness of God's existence in creation as the first angel proclaimed in Revelation 14:6-7? What keeps other people from seeing that witness?

4. Wiersbe says that God's love is a holy love rather than a love based on sentimentality. In what ways should our own love be like God's?

5. What makes it difficult to remember that it's better to "endure persecution patiently now than to escape it and suffer throughout eternity"?

6. Music is such a big piece of the picture that is painted here of heaven. What is it about music that makes it such a great tool for worship?

7. What do you think will be the most difficult parts of the choice to take the mark of the beast?

8. What underground ways do you think those who do not take that mark will use to get what they need?

Chapter Ten

Desolation and Destruction
(Revelation 17-18)

1. In what ways does the symbolism of Revelation help it to communicate to each generation?

2. How would you describe a city that could be called a harlot?

3. Give examples of this statement, "When dictators are friendly with religion, it is usually a sign that they want to make use of religion's influence and then destroy it."

4. On a scale of 1-10, "1" meaning "very separate" and "10" meaning "not separate at all," respond to this question: How separate is today's Church from governmental regulation and control?

5. What kind of idolatry to you consider to be the most tempting?

6. What cities in our nation would be the Babylons, in that their destruction would affect us all on every level?

7. In your opinion, what would be the most devastating ramification in our society if our economy was suddenly destroyed as it will be in the destruction of Babylon?

8. What does it mean to you that while you know this world will die a slow and painful death, you have another home prepared for you?

Chapter Eleven

The King and His Kingdom
(Revelation 19–20)

1. Wiersbe points out that the song of rejoicing was about God's attributes rather than Babylon's fall. In what ways can we worship God for who He is rather than what He's done for us?

2. If the bride of Christ is clothed in her acts of righteousness, how would you describe your church's state of dress?

3. How does the fact that Jesus is King of kings and Lord of lords affect our everyday choices and decisions as well as our future hope?

4. One day we could be fighting beside Jesus in a great army against evil. How are we doing that even now?

5. Wiersbe mentions the word *utopia* in conjunction with the millennial reign of Christ. Describe a world that would, to you, be a utopia.

6. Since the period of the millennium will be a golden age, what are your reactions to the fact that even in that environment, not everyone will honor God?

7. Even now, in our less-than-perfect society, what causes us to forget God's faithfulness after He has helped us so often?

8. What makes it difficult to remember during our daily lives that each action will one day be judged?

9. How can we prepare for this last and final judgment?

C h a p t e r   T w e l v e

All Things New!
(R e v e l a t i o n   2 1 – 2 2)

1. What will you most look forward to doing without when we have a new heaven and new earth?

2. How do you think our fellowship with God will be different in this new world?

3. Wiersbe says that " 'secular' and 'sacred' will be indistinguishable in heaven." On a practical level, how will that be different for us?

4. Most of us have had at least one experience where we especially felt the presence of God. Describe what it would be like to live in a place where that experience was an every-day, every-minute occurrence.

5. What kind of activities would you LIKE to have happen in heaven?

6. Give some examples of how we might "tamper" with the Word of God.

7. How would you describe the balance between waiting eagerly for the Lord's return and faithfully working until then?

8. Revelation reminds us that sin really does not go unpunished in the long run. What ramifications does that have for our lives in terms of the evil we see around us and the evil we see inside of us?

9. How can we help each other prepare for the Lord's return?